HYMNAL

HYMNAL
for Catholic Students

GIA PUBLICATIONS, INC.
CHICAGO

LITURGY TRAINING PUBLICATIONS
CHICAGO

Published with ecclesiastical approval, Archdiocese of Chicago.

Editorial committee: Robert J. Batastini, Gabe Huck, Robert H.
Oldershaw, Mary Prete, Diana Kodner Sotak, Michael Silhavy.

Design by Jane Kremsreiter. Art by Helen Siegl.

ISBN 0-941050-16-5

Contents

...

Daily Prayer

Prayer to Begin the Day

We make the sign of the cross as the leader begins:

Lord, open my lips.

Assembly:

And my mouth will proclaim your praise.

All:

Glory to the Father, and to the Son, and to the Holy Spirit:
as it was in the beginning, is now and will be for ever.
Amen. (*Outside Lent:* Alleluia).

Morning Hymn

1. This day God gives me Strength of high heav - en,
2. This day God sends me Strength as my guard - ian,
3. God's way is my way, God's shield is round me,
4. Ris - ing, I thank you, Might - y and strong One,

Sun and moon shin - ing, Flame in my hearth,
Might to up - hold me, Wis - dom as guide.
God's host de - fends me, Sav - ing from ill.
King of cre - a - tion, Giv - er of rest,

Flash - ing of light - ning, Wind in its swift - ness,
Your eyes are watch - ful, Your ears are lis - t'ning,
An - gels of heav - en, Drive from me al - ways
Firm - ly con - fess - ing Three-ness of Per - sons,

Deeps of the o - cean, Firm - ness of earth.
Your lips are speak - ing, Friend at my side.
All that would harm me, Stand by me still.
One - ness of God - head, Trin - i - ty blest.

Text: Ascr. to St. Patrick, 372-466; Adapted by James Quinn, SJ, b.1919, © 1969
Tune: BUNESSAN 5 5 5 4 D; Gaelic; Harm. by A. Gregory Murray, OSB, b.1905, ©

Psalmody

Psalm 146

Antiphon

I will praise the Lord all my days, make
mu-sic to my God while I live, make
mu-sic to my God while I live.

My soul, give praise to the Lord;
I will praise the Lord all my days,
make music to my God while I live.

Put no trust in the powerful,
mere mortals in whom there is no help.
Take their breath, they return to clay
and their plans that day come to nothing.

They are happy who are helped by Jacob's God,
whose hope is in the Lord their God,
who alone made heaven and earth,
the seas and all they contain.

It is the Lord who keeps faith for ever,
who is just to the oppressed.
It is God who gives bread to the hungry,
the Lord, who sets prisoners free,

the Lord who gives sight to the blind,
who raises up those who are bowed down,
the Lord, who protects the stranger
and upholds the widow and orphan.

It is the Lord who loves the just
but thwarts the path of the wicked.
The Lord will reign for ever,
Zion's God, from age to age.

Give praise to the Father almighty,
to the Son, Jesus Christ, our Lord,
to the Spirit who dwells in our hearts,
both now and for ever. Amen.

Psalm Prayer

Leader:

O God,
maker of the heavens and the earth,
maker of night and of day,
we sing and pray to you.
Help us to walk together in your path
and to care for one another
all through this day.
Hear our prayer through Jesus Christ our Lord.

All:

Amen.

The Word of God

The reading is from the Bible. One of the texts below may be read, or one from pages 219–21, or one chosen especially for this day.

■ Listen to the words of Paul.
  Whatever you do, in word or in deed, do everything in the name of the Lord Jesus, giving thanks to God the Father through him.
  COLOSSIANS 3:17

■ Listen to the words of the second letter of Peter.
  Grow in grace and in the knowledge of our Lord and savior Jesus Christ. To him be glory now and to the day of eternity.
  2 PETER 3:18

The reader concludes:

This is the Word of the Lord.

All:

Thanks be to God.

Canticle of Zachary

1. Blest be the God of Is - ra - el, who comes to set us free; Who vis - its and re-deems us, who grants us lib - er - ty. The proph - ets spoke of mer - cy, of free - dom and re - lease; God shall ful - fill that prom - ise and bring the peo - ple peace.

2. God, from the house of Da - vid, a child of grace has given; A sav - ior comes a-mong us to raise us up to heaven. Be-fore him goes the her - ald, fore-run - ner in the way, The proph - et of sal-va - tion, the har - bin - ger of Day.

3. On pris - on - ers of dark - ness the sun be - gins to rise, The dawn-ing of for-give - ness up - on the sin - ner's eyes. God guides the feet of pil - grims a-long the paths of peace. O bless our God and Sav - ior with songs that nev - er cease.

Text: *Canticle of Zachary;* Luke 2:68-79; Adapted by James Quinn, ©1969
Tune: ELLACOMBE, 76 76 D; *Gesangbuch der Herzogl,* Wirtenberg, 1784

8

Intercessions

Leader:

That we may walk in the light of Christ this day,
let us pray to the Lord.

All:

Lord, hear our prayer.

Leader:

That our day may be filled with charity,
   eagerness and peace,
let us pray to the Lord.

All:

Lord, hear our prayer.

Leader:

That our work and our play may bring glory to God,
let us pray to the Lord.

All:

Lord, hear our prayer.

Leader:

For the poor, the sick, and all who suffer;
for prisoners and all who are in danger,
let us pray to the Lord.

All:

Lord, hear our prayer.

Other petitions may be offered aloud or in silence.

Our Father

Leader:

Now let us pray as Jesus taught us:

All:

- Our Father, who art in heaven,
  hallowed be thy name;
  thy kingdom come;
  thy will be done on earth as it is in heaven.
  Give us this day our daily bread;
  and forgive us our trespasses
  as we forgive those who trespass against us;
  and lead us not into temptation,
  but deliver us from evil.

- Our Father in heaven,
  hallowed be your name,
  your kingdom come,
  your will be done, on earth as in heaven.
  Give us today our daily bread.
  Forgive us our sins
  as we forgive those who sin against us.
  Save us from the time of trial
  and deliver us from evil.

Concluding Prayer

Leader:

God of light,
yours is the morning
and yours is the evening.
May Jesus, the Sun of Justice,
shine for ever in our hearts
and in all that we do.
We ask this through Christ our Lord.

All:

Amen.

Blessing

Leader:

May the Lord bless us,
protect us from all evil
and bring us to everlasting life.

All:

Amen.

Prayer to End the Day

We make the sign of the cross as the leader begins:

God, come to my assistance.

Assembly:

Lord, make haste to help me.

All:

Glory to the Father, and to the Son, and to the Holy Spirit: as it was in the beginning, is now and will be for ever. Amen. (*Outside Lent:* Alleluia).

Evening Hymn

1. O ra - diant Light, O Sun di - vine Of God the
2. O Son of God, the source of life, Praise is your
3. Lord Je - sus Christ, as day - light fades, As shine the

Fa- ther's death-less face, O im - age of the Light sub-
due by night and day. Our hap- py lips must raise the
lights of e - ven - tide, We praise the Fa-ther with the

lime That fills the heav'n - ly dwell - ing place.
strain Of your es - teemed and splen - did name.
Son, The Spir - it blest, and with them one.

Text: *Phos Hilaron,* Greek, c.200; trans. by William G. Storey, b.1923, ©
Tune: JESU DULCIS MEMORIA, LM; Mode I; Acc. by Richard Proulx, b.1937
    © 1975, GIA Publications, Inc.

Psalmody

Psalm 121

Antiphon

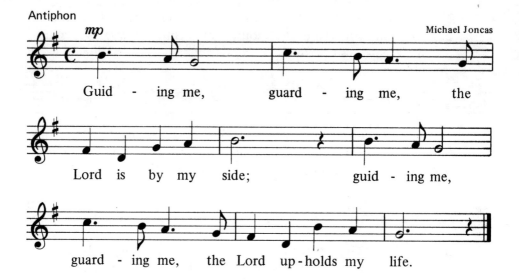

Michael Joncas

Guid - ing me, guard - ing me, the Lord is by my side; guid - ing me, guard - ing me, the Lord up - holds my life.

I lift my eyes to the mountains;
from where shall come my help?
My help shall come from the Lord my God
who made heaven and earth.

May he never allow you to stumble!
Let him sleep not, your guard.
No, he sleeps not nor slumbers,
he, Israel's guard.

The Lord is your guard and your shade;
at your right side he stands.
By day the sun shall not smite you
nor the moon in the night.

The Lord will guard you from evil,
he will guard your soul.
The Lord will guard your going and coming
both now and for ever.

Praise the Father, the Son and Holy Spirit,
both now and for ever,
the God who is, who was and who will be,
world without end.

Psalm Prayer

Leader:

Lord God,
every day and every night
you watch over our coming and our going.
Protect us from danger
and lead us safely home to you.
You are good and you love us for ever and ever.

All:

Amen.

The Word of God

The reading is from the Bible. One of the texts below may be read,
or one from pages 222–24, or one chosen especially for this day.

■ Listen to the words of the gospel of Luke.
As they approached the village to which they were
going, Jesus gave the impression that he was going on
farther. But they urged him, "Stay with us, for it is nearly
evening and the day is almost over." So he went in to
stay with them.
LUKE 24:28–29

■ Listen to the words of Paul.
Be on your guard, stand firm in the faith, be courageous,
be strong. Your every act should be done with love. The
grace of the Lord Jesus be with you. My love to all of
you in Christ Jesus.
1 CORINTHIANS 16:13–14, 23–24

The reader concludes:

This is the Word of the Lord.

Assembly:

Thanks be to God.

Canticle of Mary

1. My soul gives glo - ry to the Lord, In
2. His mer - cy goes to all who fear, From
3. He raised his ser - vant Is - ra - el, Re-

God my Sav - ior I re - joice. My
age to age and to all parts. His
mem - b'ring his e - ter - nal grace, As

low - li - ness he did re - gard, Ex-
arm of strength to all is near; He
from of old he did fore - tell To

alt - ing me by his own choice.
scat - ters those who have proud hearts.
A - bra - ham and all his race.

From this day all shall call me blest, For
He casts the might - y from their throne And
O Fa -ther, Son and Spir - it blest, In

he has done great things for me, Of
rais - es those of low de - gree; He
three - fold Name are you a - dored, To

all great names his is the best, For
feeds the hun - gry as his own, The
you be ev - 'ry prayer ad - drest, From

it is ho - ly; strong is he.
rich de - part in pov - er - ty.
age to age the on - ly Lord.

Text: *Magnificat Anima Mea,* Luke 1:46-55; trans. by John T. Mueller
Tune: MAGNIFICAT, LMD; Michael Joncas, b.1951, © 1979, GIA Publications, Inc.

Intercessions

Leader:

For the church,
let us pray to the Lord.

Assembly:

Lord, hear our prayer.

Leader:

For all who serve in government,
let us pray to the Lord.

Assembly:

Lord, hear our prayer.

Leader:

For the poor, the sick, the lonely and the sorrowful,
let us pray to the Lord.

Assembly:

Lord, hear our prayer.

Leader:

For peace in the world,
let us pray to the Lord.

Assembly:

Lord, hear our prayer.

Other prayers may be offered aloud or in silence, always concluding:

For all who have died,
let us pray to the Lord.

Assembly:

Lord, hear our prayer.

Our Father

Leader:

Now let us pray as Jesus taught us:

All:

- Our Father, who art in heaven,
  hallowed be thy name;
  thy kingdom come;
  thy will be done on earth as it is in heaven.
  Give us this day our daily bread;
  and forgive us our trespasses
  as we forgive those who trespass against us;
  and lead us not into temptation,
  but deliver us from evil.

- Our Father in heaven,
  hallowed be your name,
  your kingdom come,
  your will be done, on earth as in heaven.
  Give us today our daily bread.
  Forgive us our sins
  as we forgive those who sin against us.
  Save us from the time of trial
  and deliver us from evil.

Concluding Prayer

Leader:

Be our shining light, O Lord,
during the rest of this day
and all through the night.
Show us the good that surrounds us
so that we might praise you.
Protect us from all dangers
that we might give you thanks
through Jesus, who is Lord for ever and ever.

All:

Amen.

Blessing

Leader:

May the Lord bless us,
protect us from all evil
and bring us to everlasting life.

All:

Amen.

■ ■ ■

Mass

Sunday Mass

Introductory Rites

To begin, we join in songs and prayers. In this way we draw near to the reading of God's word and to the eucharist. Some of the following parts will always be included.

Greeting

We make the sign of the cross as the priest begins:

In the name of the Father, and of the Son,
  and of the Holy Spirit.

Assembly:

Amen.

The priest greets everyone with these or other words:

The Lord be with you.

Assembly:

And also with you.

Water may now be blessed and sprinkled on all to remind us of our baptism, or the penitential rite is celebrated.

Penitential Rite

We remember how much we are loved by God and so we pray for forgiveness of sins and we praise God's mercy. The penitential rite may include either the following prayer or a litany. In this prayer, we strike our breast as a mark of sorrow, at the words "through my own fault."

I confess to almighty God,
and to you, my brothers and sisters,
that I have sinned through my own fault
in my thoughts and in my words,
in what I have done,
and in what I have failed to do;
and I ask blessed Mary, ever virgin,
all the angels and saints,
and you, my brothers and sisters,
to pray for me to the Lord our God.

The priest or the cantor leads us in saying or singing:

■ Lord, have mercy.
  Christ, have mercy.
  Lord, have mercy.

■ Kyrie eleison.
  Christe eleison.
  Kyrie eleison.

Gloria

On most Sundays we sing this ancient hymn of praise.

Glory to God in the highest,
   and peace to his people on earth.

Lord God, heavenly King,
almighty God and Father,
   we worship you, we give you thanks,
   we praise you for your glory.

Lord Jesus Christ, only Son of the Father,
Lord God, Lamb of God,
you take away the sin of the world:
   have mercy on us;
you are seated at the right hand of the Father:
   receive our prayer.

For you alone are the Holy One,
you alone are the Lord,
you alone are the Most High,
   Jesus Christ,
   with the Holy Spirit,
   in the glory of God the Father. Amen.

Opening Prayer

The priest says "Let us pray." We pray in silence and then respond
"Amen" to the prayer spoken by the priest.

Liturgy of the Word

First and Second Readings

Whenever the church gathers, the scriptures are read. Usually on Sundays we listen to three readings. These are God's word spoken to us, the church. That is why the reader concludes the first readings by saying:

This is the Word of the Lord.

And we respond:

Thanks be to God.

Usually there is a time of silence after a reading so that we can think about what we have heard. Between the first reading and the second reading, we join in singing the verse of a psalm. Psalms are prayers and songs from the Bible.

Gospel

Before the gospel, we prepare by singing "Alleluia," a Hebrew word that means "Praise the Lord." During Lent, instead of "Alleluia," we sing "Praise to you, Lord Jesus Christ, king of endless glory" or "Glory and praise to you, Lord Jesus Christ."

The deacon (or priest) begins:

The Lord be with you.

Assembly:

And also with you.

Deacon (Priest):

A reading from the holy gospel according to (Matthew, Mark, Luke or John).

*We make a small sign of the cross on forehead, lips and heart, and
we answer:*

Glory to you, Lord.

After the gospel, the deacon (priest) kisses the book and says:

This is the Gospel of the Lord.

Assembly:

Praise to you, Lord Jesus Christ.

Homily

The priest speaks to us about the word of God.

Profession of Faith

On Sundays, we recite again the faith we professed at our baptism.

- We believe in one God,
  the Father, the Almighty,
  maker of heaven and earth,
  of all that is seen and unseen.

  We believe in one Lord, Jesus Christ,
  the only Son of God,
  eternally begotten of the Father,
  God from God, Light from Light,
  true God from true God,
  begotten, not made, one in Being with the Father.
  Through him all things were made.
  For us men and for our salvation he came down
      from heaven:

All bow during the next two lines:

by the power of the Holy Spirit
   he was born of the Virgin Mary, and became man.
For our sake he was crucified under Pontius Pilate;
   he suffered, died, and was buried.
On the third day he rose again
    in fulfillment of the Scriptures;
   he ascended into heaven
    and is seated at the right hand of the Father.
He will come again in glory to judge the living
   and the dead,
   and his kingdom will have no end.

We believe in the Holy Spirit, the Lord, the giver of life,
   who proceeds from the Father and the Son.
With the Father and the Son he is worshiped
   and glorified.
He has spoken through the Prophets.
We believe in one holy catholic and apostolic Church.
We acknowledge one baptism for the forgiveness of
   sins.
We look for the resurrection of the dead,
   and the life of the world to come. Amen.

Sometimes the Apostles' Creed is used instead:

■ We believe in God, the Father almighty,
   creator of heaven and earth.

We believe in Jesus Christ, his only Son, our Lord.
   He was conceived by the power of the Holy Spirit
   and born of the Virgin Mary.
   He suffered under Pontius Pilate,
    was crucified, died, and was buried.
   He descended to the dead.
   On the third day he arose again.

He ascended into heaven,
and is seated at the right hand of the Father.
He will come again to judge the living and the dead.

We believe in the Holy Spirit,
the holy catholic Church,
the communion of saints,
the forgiveness of sins,
the resurrection of the body,
and the life everlasting. Amen.

General Intercessions

In the intercessions, we pray for all the world: for the church, for leaders, for the poor and all in need, for the sick and for the dead. Usually we respond "Lord, hear our prayer" or "Lord, have mercy" to each intercession.

Liturgy of the Eucharist

Preparation of the Altar and the Gifts

Bread and wine, "fruit of the earth and work of human hands," are now brought to the table. The deacon or priest prepares these gifts. If the prayers are said aloud, we respond "Blessed be God for ever." After the table is prepared, the priest invites us to pray and we respond:

May the Lord accept the sacrifice at your hands
for the praise and glory of his name,
for our good, and the good of all his Church.

We stand. The priest says the prayer over the gifts and we respond by saying "Amen."

✠

Eucharistic Prayer

We now give full attention to the prayer that is the center of the Mass.

Priest:

The Lord be with you.

Assembly:

And also with you.

Priest:

Lift up your hearts.

Assembly:

We lift them up to the Lord.

Priest:

Let us give thanks to the Lord our God.

Assembly:

It is right to give him thanks and praise.

The priest invites us to join the angels and all creation in praising God. We sing:

Holy, holy, holy Lord, God of power and might.
Heaven and earth are full of your glory.
　Hosanna in the highest.
Blessed is he who comes in the name of the Lord.
　Hosanna in the highest.

The eucharistic prayer continues. The priest praises God and asks God to send the Holy Spirit upon us and our gifts. The priest remembers how Jesus gave his friends bread and wine, saying: "Take

and eat, this is my body. Take and drink, this is the cup of my blood."
Then the priest invites us to proclaim the mystery of faith, and we
respond with one of the following acclamations:

- Christ has died,
  Christ is risen,
  Christ will come again.

- Dying you destroyed our death,
  rising you restored our life.
  Lord Jesus, come in glory.

- When we eat this bread and drink this cup,
  we proclaim your death, Lord Jesus,
  until you come in glory.

- Lord, by your cross and resurrection
  you have set us free.
  You are the Savior of the world.

At the end of the eucharistic prayer, the priest lifts up the holy bread
and cup and proclaims that through Jesus and in the unity of the
Holy Spirit, all glory belongs to God for ever and ever. We sing
"Amen" to this, sometimes repeating our "Amen" (which means "Yes"
or "So be it") many times.

Communion Rite

Lord's Prayer

The priest invites us to pray as Jesus taught us.

Our Father, who art in heaven,
hallowed be thy name;
thy kingdom come;
thy will be done on earth as it is in heaven.
Give us this day our daily bread;

and forgive us our trespasses
as we forgive those who trespass against us;
and lead us not into temptation,
but deliver us from evil.

The priest continues the prayer and all join to conclude:

For the kingdom, the power, and the glory are yours,
   now and for ever.

Sign of Peace

The priest prays for peace and then greets the assembly:

The peace of the Lord be with you always.

Assembly:

And also with you.

The deacon or priest then invites us to exchange a sign of Christ's peace with those around us.

Breaking of the Bread

The priest lifts up the holy bread and breaks it so that all may share the body of Christ in holy communion. While the bread is being broken and cups poured for communion, we sing:

Lamb of God, you take away the sins of the world:
   have mercy on us.

This is repeated until the bread and cups are prepared and we conclude:

Lamb of God, you take away the sins of the world:
   grant us peace.

Communion

The priest invites us to holy communion, saying "Happy are those who are called to his supper." We respond:

Lord, I am not worthy to receive you,
but only say the word and I shall be healed.

Each person comes forward in the procession, singing the communion song. The minister of communion says to us:

The body of Christ.
The blood of Christ.

We respond:

Amen.

We keep a silent time after all have come to communion. There is a final prayer to which we respond "Amen."

Concluding Rite

Blessing

The priest gives the blessing and all make the sign of the cross. We respond "Amen."

Dismissal

The deacon or the priest dismisses the assembly and we respond "Thanks be to God." A song may be sung.

Mass on Other Days

Like Mass on Sunday, Mass on other days has two parts. The first is called the liturgy of the word. This is the time when we listen to readings from the Bible, sing psalms and alleluias, and join in prayers for all that the world needs.

The second part of Mass is called the liturgy of the eucharist. "Eucharist" means "giving thanks." For us, it means giving thanks at the holy table where bread and wine have been prepared. Led by the priest, we give thanks to God for all the ways that God has loved our world. Especially we give thanks for Jesus who spoke to us about God and showed us God's love in his life, his death and his resurrection. We call on the Holy Spirit to come that the bread and wine might become for us the body and the blood of our Lord Jesus Christ. Then we are invited to come to the table and to share this holy food.

The word and the eucharist are what we do whenever we celebrate the Mass. Before the liturgy of the word, the introductory rites help us to gather together as the church. After the liturgy of the eucharist, we are blessed and sent out to live as Christians.

If we look at the actions of the Mass, this is what we see:

- First, we gather together. Often we do this with song and with the sign of the cross and with prayer.

- Next we listen to God's word in the Bible. We sing psalms and alleluias and have some silent time for thinking about God's word. We pray for all the world.

- Then we prepare the table with bread and wine. We join in singing thanks to God, in praying the Our Father, in the greeting of peace and in holy communion.

- At the end of Mass we go out to bring everyone the love of God we have found together.

Introductory Rites

We should know these words and actions by heart. Some of them will be part of our time of gathering together.

- Amen.

  We use this word at the end of the sign of the cross and at the end of the prayers. It is a word from the language Jesus spoke and it means "Yes," "So be it."

- And also with you.

  This is our answer when the priest greets us.

- I confess to almighty God,
  and to you, my brothers and sisters,
  that I have sinned through my own fault
  in my thoughts and in my words,
  in what I have done,
  and in what I have failed to do;
  and I ask blessed Mary, ever virgin,
  all the angels and saints,
  and you, my brothers and sisters,
  to pray for me to the Lord our God.

*We use these words to remember how we sometimes fail to love God
and one another, and to remember how we are surrounded by saints
and angels who are our friends. This is also a good prayer to use at
the end of the day before going to bed. At the words "through my
own fault," we strike our breast as a mark of sorrow.*

- Lord, have mercy.
  Christ, have mercy.
  Lord, have mercy.

- Kyrie eleison.
  Christe eleison.
  Kyrie eleison.

*A litany is a way of praying when we repeat one thing over and over.
This is a short litany of praise for the mercy we find in Jesus.
Sometimes it is prayed in Greek.*

*The Gloria on page 27 will sometimes be sung or recited on feast
days. This is another prayer to know by heart.*

Liturgy of the Word

Reading

*There are usually two readings from the Bible. We listen to them
closely. At the end of the reading, the reader says "This is the
Word of the Lord." We know our response to that by heart:*

Thanks be to God.

Psalm

After a reading, we usually have a silent time to think about what we have heard. Between the readings, we often sing a psalm. A psalm is a prayer from the Bible. Usually we sing just one line, then the leader sings or reads several verses of the psalm. Then we sing our line again. Our part is called the "psalm refrain" because it is repeated several times. Some of these psalm refrains are on pages 55–65. Because the refrains are so short, we usually come to know them by heart.

Gospel

The gospel is the last reading. This is a story about Jesus or it is some words that Jesus spoke or a story Jesus told. To prepare for the gospel we stand and sing and give our attention.

Al - le - lu - ia,   al - le - lu- ia,   al - le - lu - ia.

During the days of Lent, we do not sing the joyful alleluia. Instead we welcome the gospel with these words:

Praise to you, Lord   Je - sus Christ, king of end-less glo-ry!

When the deacon (or priest) announces "A reading from the holy gospel," we make a small sign of the cross on forehead, lips and heart, and we answer:

Glory to you, Lord.

After the gospel, the reader kisses the book and says "This is the Gospel of the Lord." We respond:

Praise to you, Lord Jesus Christ.

Homily

After the gospel, someone speaks with us about God's word and our lives. On great feast days, we may then join in the Profession of Faith (on page 29, or page 30 for the Apostles' Creed).

General Intercessions

This is another litany prayer. One after another, we pray for the needs of the church and the world and for our own needs. Each time we respond, usually with one of these short prayers:

- Lord, hear our prayer.

- Lord, have mercy.

- Kyrie eleison.

Our response may be sung:

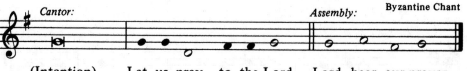

Cantor: Assembly: **Byzantine Chant**

(Intention)   Let us pray   to the Lord.   Lord, hear our prayer.

Liturgy of the Eucharist

Preparation of the Altar and the Gifts

Our bread and wine are placed on the table we call the altar. Sometimes we join in saying "Blessed be God for ever."

When all is ready, we say together:

May the Lord accept the sacrifice at your hands
for the praise and glory of his name,
for our good, and the good of all his Church.

Eucharistic Prayer

We are led by the priest in giving thanks and praise to God. All the responses and acclamations we are to know by heart. We begin by answering the invitation of the priest:

The Lord be with you.

Assembly:

And also with you.

Priest:

Lift up your hearts.

Assembly:

We lift them up to the Lord.

Priest:

Let us give thanks to the Lord our God.

Assembly:

It is right to give him thanks and praise.

The priest then speaks or sings our thanks to God and we join all creation in this song of praise:

"A Community Mass"
Richard Proulx, 1970

mf

Ho- ly, ho - ly, ho - ly Lord, God of pow-er and might, heav'n and earth are full of your glo - ry. Ho - san - na in the high-est, ho - san- na in the high - est. Blest is he who comes in the name of the Lord. Ho - san - na in the high-est, ho - san - na in the high - est.

The eucharistic prayer continues. Sometimes we join in short songs of acclamation and praise many times as the priest asks God to send the Holy Spirit upon us and our gifts. The priest remembers how Jesus gave his friends bread and wine, saying: "Take and eat, this is my body. Take and drink, this is the cup of my blood." Then the priest invites us to proclaim the mystery of faith, and we respond:

Richard Proulx

When we eat this bread and drink this cup, we pro-claim your death, Lord Je-sus, un-til you come in glo-ry.

At the end of the eucharistic prayer, the priest lifts up the holy bread and cup and proclaims that through Jesus and in the unity of the Holy Spirit, all glory belongs to God the Father for ever and ever. We sing our "Amen" to this:

Danish

A - men, a - men, a - men.

Communion Rite

Lord's Prayer

The priest invites us to pray as Jesus taught us. Christians know the Lord's Prayer by heart and pray it every day.

Adapt. by Robert Snow, 1964

Our Fa-ther, who art in heav - en, hal-lowed be thy name;

thy king-dom come; thy will be done on earth as it is in

heav - en. Give us this day our dai-ly bread; and for - give

us our tres-pass - es as we for - give those who tres-pass a-

gainst us; and lead us not in - to temp- ta - tion,

but de - liv - er us from e - vil.

The priest continues the prayer and all join to conclude:

For the king - dom, the pow'r, and the
glo - ry are yours, now and for ev - er.

Sign of Peace

The priest prays for peace and then greets the assembly:

The peace of the Lord be with you always.

Assembly:

And also with you.

*The priest then asks us to exchange a sign of Christ's peace with
those around us. In making peace, we prepare for holy communion.*

Breaking of the Bread

*Then the priest lifts up the holy bread and breaks it so that all may
share the body of Christ in holy communion. While the bread is being
broken and the cups poured for communion, we sing:*

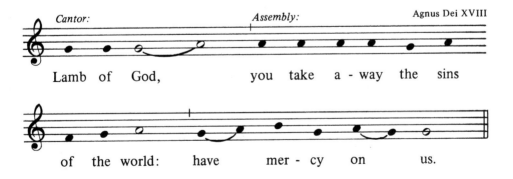

Lamb of God, you take a - way the sins
of the world: have mer - cy on us.

Agnus Dei XVIII

This is sung two or more times. When the bread and wine have been prepared, the "Lamb of God" concludes:

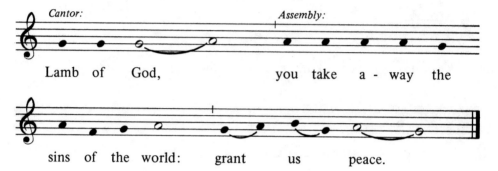

Lamb of God, you take a - way the sins of the world: grant us peace.

Communion

The priest invites us to holy communion, saying "Happy are those who are called to his supper." We respond by heart:

Lord, I am not worthy to receive you,
but only say the word and I shall be healed.

Each person comes forward in the procession, singing the communion song. The minister of communion says to us:

The body of Christ.
The blood of Christ.

We respond:

Amen.

When the communion procession is complete, we keep a silent time. Then there is a final prayer to which we respond "Amen."

Concluding Rite

Now we receive a blessing and make the sign of the cross. We answer "Amen." Then the deacon or priest announces to us that the Mass has ended and tells us to go in peace to love and serve the Lord. We respond:

Thanks be to God.

∎ ∎ ∎

Reconciliation

We are baptized people and we try to lead lives filled with kindness, lives that bring justice, lives of sharing. We often fail to keep this way we have learned as Christians. We need to seek forgiveness from God and from one another. And we need to forgive each other. This is what we pray every day in the Our Father and every Sunday at Mass.

At some times during the year, and especially during the season of Lent, Christians gather for the sacrament of reconciliation — also called the sacrament of penance. At this time we can confess our failures, we can hear God's word and find God's loving forgiveness. Afterward, we can carry that forgiveness to others. Sometimes we Christians do this by sharing our time and our goods, sometimes by learning to get along with a little less of some things and being more filled with thanks for what we have and use.

When we come together for the sacrament of reconciliation, we spend some time in quiet thought about our lives. We think of how God has blessed us, of how there have also been hard things in our lives, and of how we have sometimes sinned "in my thoughts and in my words, in what I have done, and in what I have failed to do."

Introductory Rites

The liturgy may begin with a song and the sign of the cross. The priest greets everyone and then leads the opening prayer.

The Word of God

We listen to readings from the Bible. Between the readings, we may join in singing a psalm.

Psalm 51

Patricia Craig

Be mer - ci - ful, O Lord, for we have sinned.

Psalm 91

Marty Haugen

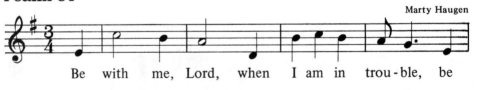

Be with me, Lord, when I am in trou - ble, be

with me, Lord, I pray.

Before the gospel, we sing the "Alleluia" or the Lenten acclamation.

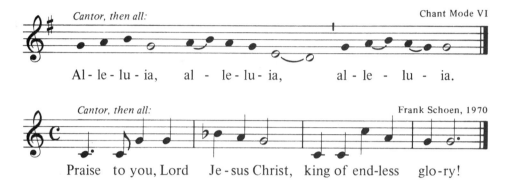

After the homily, we take time to reflect on our lives with sorrow for our sins.

Sacrament of Penance

We may kneel and join in the prayer "I confess" (page 26) or another prayer of sorrow for sin (see the Prayer of Contrition on page 218). Then we join in a litany asking for God's mercy and we pray the Our Father.

One by one, then, we approach the priest to confess our sins. The priest places his hands on each person's head in a gesture of love and forgiveness. He says a prayer that concludes: "Through the ministry of the church may God give you pardon and peace, and I absolve you from your sins in the name of the Father, and of the Son, and of the Holy Spirit." Each person responds "Amen."

When everyone is ready, all join in singing a hymn of praise to God who has shown us such mercy.

. . .

Psalm Refrains

Psalm 15

Richard Proulx

Those who do jus - tice will live in the pres - ence of the Lord.

Psalm 23

Joseph Gelineau

My shep-herd is the Lord, noth-ing in-deed shall I want.

Psalm 23

A. Gregory Murray

The Lord is my shep - herd, noth-ing shall I want: he leads me by safe paths, noth-ing shall I fear.

Psalm 24

J. Robert Carroll

Lord, this is the peo-ple that longs to see your face.

Psalm 25

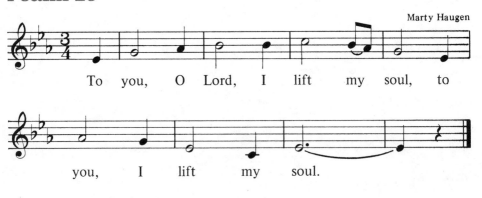

Marty Haugen

To you, O Lord, I lift my soul, to you, I lift my soul.

Psalm 27

David Haas

The Lord is my light and my sal-va-tion, of whom should I be a - fraid?

Psalm 33

Columba Kelly

Hap - py the peo - ple the Lord has cho - sen to be his own.

Psalm 34

Richard Proulx

Taste and see the good-ness of the Lord, taste and see.

59

Psalm 47

Robert Kreutz

God mounts his throne, to shouts of joy; a blare of trum - pets for the Lord.

Psalm 51

Patricia Craig

Be mer - ci - ful, O Lord, for we have sinned.

Psalm 78

Robert J. Batastini

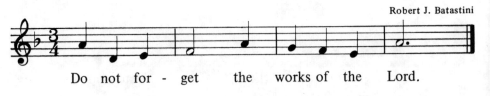

Do not for - get the works of the Lord.

Psalm 84

A. Gregory Murray

How love - ly is your dwell-ing place, O Lord of hosts.

Psalm 91

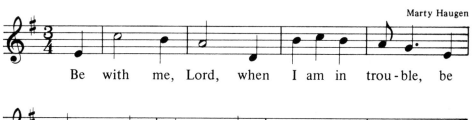

Marty Haugen

Be with me, Lord, when I am in trou - ble, be

with me, Lord, I pray.

Psalm 96

Joseph Gelineau

Great is the Lord, wor - thy of praise; tell all the na-tions

"God is King"; spread the news of his love.

Psalm 96

Clifford W. Howell

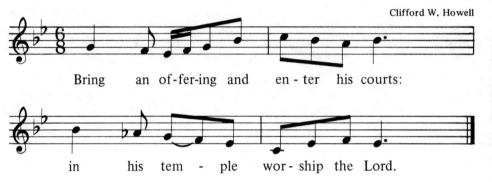

Bring an of-fer-ing and en - ter his courts: in his tem - ple wor - ship the Lord.

Psalm 98

J. Robert Carroll

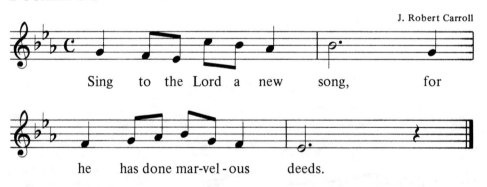

Sing to the Lord a new song, for he has done mar-vel - ous deeds.

Psalm 98

David Haas/Marty Haugen

All the ends of the earth have seen the pow-er of God; all the ends of the earth have seen the pow-er of God.

Psalm 104

David Haas

Lord, send out your Spir - it, and re - new the face of the earth; Lord, send out your Spir-it, and re - new the face of the earth.

Psalm 114

Richard Proulx

God has freed us and re-deemed us with his might - y arm.

Psalm 118

Richard Proulx

1. This is the day the Lord has made; let us re-joice, let us re-joice,
2. let us re-joice and be glad.

Psalm 122

A. Gregory Murray

We shall go up with joy to the house of our God.

Psalm 138

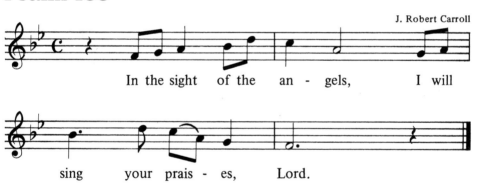

J. Robert Carroll

In the sight of the an - gels, I will sing your prais - es, Lord.

. . .

Acclamations and Litanies

Rite of Sprinkling

"Festival Liturgy"
Richard Hillert, 1983

Moderately slow

Lord Je-sus, from your wound-ed side flowed streams of cleans-ing wa-ter. Al- le- lu - ia, al - le- lu - ia, al - le - lu - ia. The world was washed of all its sin, all life made new a-gain. Al- le- lu - ia, al- le - lu- ia, al - le - lu - ia.

Kyrie

"Deutsche Mass"
Franz Schubert, 1826
Adapt. by Richard Proulx, 1985

Lord, have mer - cy. Lord, have mer - cy. Christ, have mer - cy. Christ, have mer - cy. Lord, have mer - cy. Lord, have mer - cy. Lord, have mer - cy, have mer - cy.

Kyrie

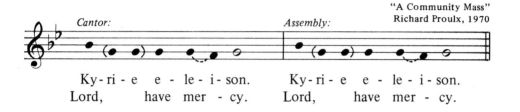

Cantor: *Assembly:*   "A Community Mass"
Richard Proulx, 1970

Ky - ri - e e - le - i - son. Ky - ri - e e - le - i - son.
Lord, have mer - cy.   Lord, have mer - cy.

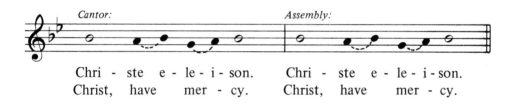

Chri - ste e - le - i - son. Chri - ste e - le - i - son.
Christ, have mer - cy.   Christ, have mer - cy.

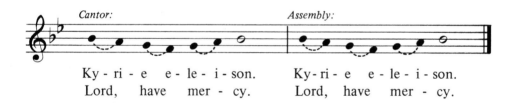

Ky - ri - e e - le - i - son. Ky - ri - e e - le - i - son.
Lord, have mer - cy.   Lord, have mer - cy.

Gloria

"A New Mass for Congregations"
Carroll T. Andrews, 1970

Glo - ry to God in the high - est, and

peace to his peo - ple on earth. Lord God,

heav - en - ly King, al - might - y God and

Fa - ther, we wor - ship you, we give you thanks, we

praise you for your glo - ry.

Lord Je - sus Christ, on - ly Son of the Fa - ther,

Lord God, Lamb of God, you take a - way the

sin of the world: have mer - cy on

us; you are seat - ed at the right hand of the

Fa - ther: re - ceive our prayer.

f tempo primo

For you a - lone are the Ho - ly One,

you a - lone are the Lord, you a - lone are the

Most High, Je - sus Christ, with the Ho - ly Spir - it,

ff *rit.*

in the glo - ry of God the Fa - ther. A - men.

Gloria

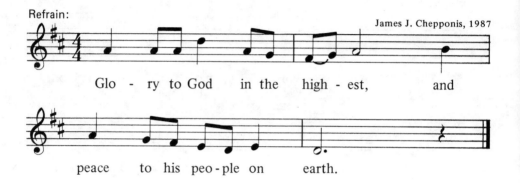

Refrain:

James J. Chepponis, 1987

Glo - ry to God in the high - est, and

peace to his peo - ple on earth.

Alleluia: Form A

Taizé Community
Jacques Berthier, 1984

Al-le - lu - ia, al-le - lu - ia, al-le - lu - ia.

Al-le - lu - ia, al-le - lu - ia, al-le - lu - ia.

Alleluia: Form B

Marty Haugen, 1987

1.　2.　3.

Al - le - lu - ia, al - le - lu - ia, al - le - lu - ia.

Alleluia: Form C

Celtic Alleluia
Fintan O'Carroll, Christopher Walker

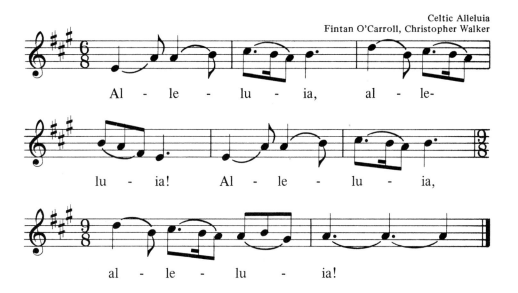

Al - le - lu - ia, al - le-
lu - ia! Al - le - lu - ia,
al - le - lu - ia!

General Intercessions

Taizé Community
Jacques Berthier, 1980

Ky-ri- e, Ky-ri-e e -le - i -son. (hum)

Sanctus

"People's Mass"
Jan Vermulst, 1970

Ho - ly, ho - ly, ho - ly Lord,
God of pow-er and might, heav - en and earth are
full of your glo - ry. Ho - san - na in the
high - est. Bless - ed is he who comes in the name of the
Lord. Ho - san - na in the high - est.

Memorial Acclamation

Charles George Frischmann, 1970

Lord, by your cross and res - ur - rec - tion,
you have set us free. You are the
Sav - ior of the world.

Preface Dialogue

"Mass of Creation"
Marty Haugen, 1984

The Lord be with you. And al - so with you.

Lift up your hearts. We lift them up to the Lord.

Let us give thanks to the Lord our God.

It is right to give him thanks and praise.

*Three different times during the Preface, the following is sung after
the priest says:*

. . . With Jesus we sing your praise:

Ho - san - na   in   the   high - est!

Sanctus

We thank you with the angels and saints as they praise you and sing:

"Mass of Creation"
Marty Haugen, 1984

f

Ho - ly,   ho - ly,   ho - ly,   Lord,

God   of   pow - er,   God   of   might,

heav - en and earth   are   filled   with your   glo - ry.

ff

Ho - san - na   in   the   high - est!

mf

Bless - ed   is   he   who   comes in   the

f   *ff*

name of   the   Lord.   Ho - san - na

rit. *fff*

in   the   high - est,   ho - san - na

in the high - est!

. . . He promised to send the Holy Spirit, to be with us always so that we can live as your children.

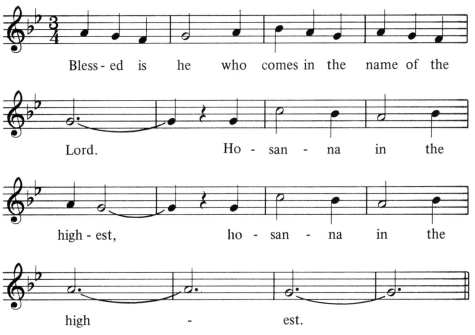

Bless - ed is he who comes in the name of the Lord. Ho - san - na in the high - est, ho - san - na in the high - est.

The following is sung after the priest shows the consecrated host to the people, and again after he shows the chalice.

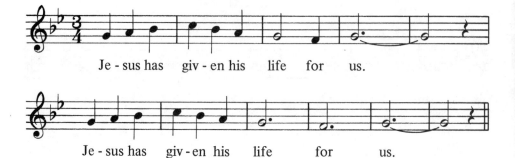

The following is sung after each of these four texts:

. . . He put himself into our hands to be the sacrifice we offer you.

. . . all other bishops, and all who serve your people.

. . . Bring them home to you to be with you for ever.

. . . friends of Jesus the Lord will sing a song of joy.

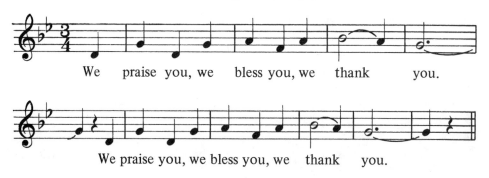

Memorial Acclamation

When the acclamations from the Second Eucharistic Prayer for Children are not used, this Memorial Acclamation is appropriate.

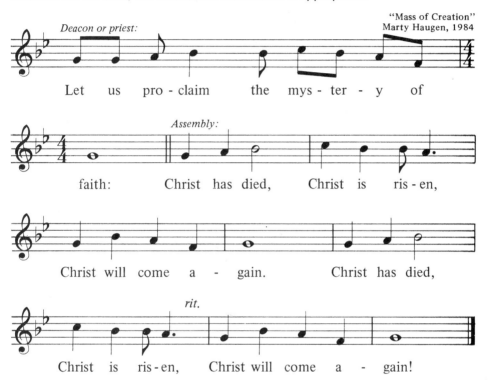

"Mass of Creation"
Marty Haugen, 1984

Deacon or priest:

Let us pro-claim the mys-ter-y of faith: Christ has died, Christ is ris-en, Christ will come a-gain. Christ has died, Christ is ris-en, Christ will come a-gain!

Assembly:

rit.

Amen

... almighty Father, for ever and ever.

"Mass of Creation"
Marty Haugen, 1984

A-men, a-men, a-men! A-men, a-men, a-men!

rit. *molto rit.*

Preface Dialogue

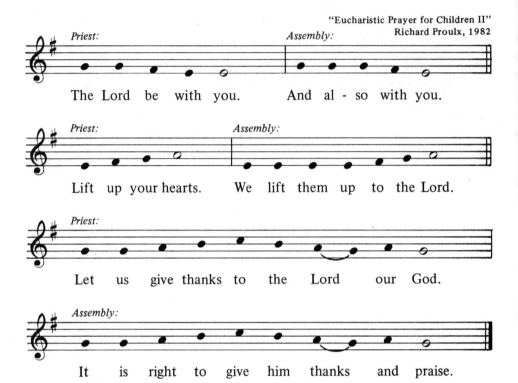

"Eucharistic Prayer for Children II"
Richard Proulx, 1982

Priest: The Lord be with you. *Assembly:* And al - so with you.

Priest: Lift up your hearts. *Assembly:* We lift them up to the Lord.

Priest: Let us give thanks to the Lord our God.

Assembly: It is right to give him thanks and praise.

Three different times during the Preface, the following is sung after the priest says:

. . . With Jesus we sing your praise:

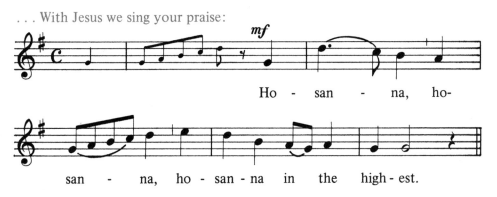

Ho - san - na, ho-san - na, ho - san - na in the high - est.

Sanctus

We thank you with the angels and saints as they praise you and sing:

Ho - ly, ho - ly, ho - ly Lord,
God of pow-er and might, heav - en and
earth are full of your glo - ry. Ho-
san - na, ho - san - na, ho - san - na in the
high - est. Ho - ly, ho - ly, ho - ly Lord,
God of pow-er and might. Bless - ed is
he who comes in the name of the

Lord. Ho - san - na, ho - san - na, ho-
san - na in the high - est.

. . . He promised to send the Holy Spirit, to be with us always so that we can live as your children.

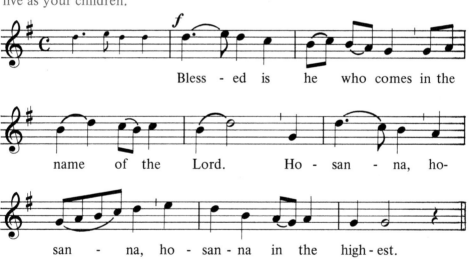

Bless - ed is he who comes in the
name of the Lord. Ho - san - na, ho-
san - na, ho - san - na in the high - est.

The following is sung as the priest shows the consecrated host to the people, and again when he shows the chalice.

Je - sus has giv - en his life for us.

The following is sung after each of these four texts:

. . . He put himself into our hands to be the sacrifice we offer you.
. . . all other bishops, and all who serve your people.
. . . Bring them home to you to be with you for ever.
. . . friends of Jesus the Lord will sing a song of joy.

We praise you, we bless you, we thank you.

Memorial Acclamation

When the acclamations from the Second Eucharistic Prayer for
Children are not used, this Memorial Acclamation is appropriate.

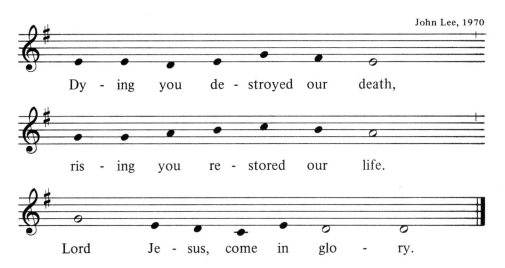

John Lee, 1970

Dy - ing you de - stroyed our death,

ris - ing you re - stored our life.

Lord Je - sus, come in glo - ry.

Amen

. . . almighty Father, for ever and ever.

"Eucharistic Prayer for Children II"
Richard Proulx, 1982

A - men, a - men,

a - men. A - men,

a - men, a - men, a - men.

A - men, a - men, a - men.

A - men, a - men, a - men.

A - men, a - men, a - men, a - men.

A - men, a - men, a - men.

* Possible endings

Lord's Prayer

"Mass of Creation"
Marty Haugen, 1984

mf

Our Fa-ther, who art in heav-en, hal-low-ed be thy name; thy king-dom come, thy will be done on earth as it is in heav-en.

Give us this day our dai-ly bread; and for-

poco rit.

give us our tres-pass-es as we for-give those who

a tempo

tres-pass a-gainst us; and lead us not in-to temp-

ta-tion, but de-liv-er us from e-vil. Presider: *(spoken)*
"Deliver us, Lord. . ."

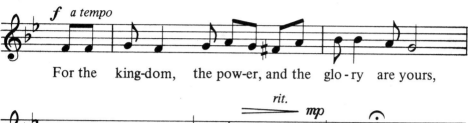

For the king-dom, the pow-er, and the glo-ry are yours,

now and for ev - er - more. A - men.

Agnus Dei

Richard Proulx, 1975

Lamb of God, you take a-way the

sins of the world: have mer - cy on us.

Lamb of God, you take a-way the sins of the

world: grant us peace, grant us peace.

Agnus Dei

"Mass of Creation"
Marty Haugen, 1984

Je - sus, ...

poco rit. All: *a tempo*

. . . . you   take a - way the   sins   of the

poco rit.

world: have   mer - cy on   us.

Last time:
Cantor: *poco rit.*   *All:*   *a tempo*

Je - sus, Lamb of   God: you   take a - way the

sins of the   world: grant us you peace.

Agnus Dei

"Holy Cross Mass"
David Clark Isele, 1979

Lamb of God, you take a - way the

sins of the world, have mer - cy on us. grant us peace.

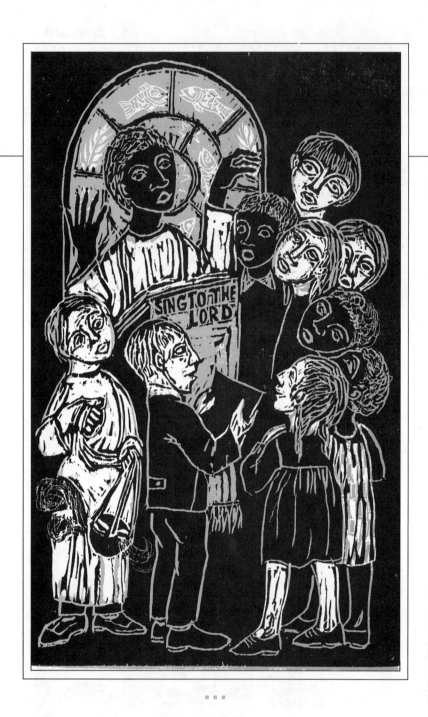

Hymns

Again We Keep This Solemn Fast

1. A - gain we keep this sol - emn fast, A
2. More spar - ing, there - fore, let us make The
3. Let us a - void each harm - ful way That
4. We pray, O bless - ed, Ho - ly One, Our

gift of faith from a - ges past, This Lent which binds us
words we speak, the food we take, Our sleep, our laugh - ter,
lures the care - less mind a - stray; By watch-ful prayer our
God while end - less a - ges run, That this, our Lent of

lov - ing - ly To faith and hope and char - i - ty.
ev - 'ry sense; Learn peace thru ho - ly pen - i - tence.
spir - its free From schem-ing of the En - e - my.
for - ty days, May bring us growth and give you praise.

Text: *Ex more docti mystico;* Ascr. to Gregory the Great, c.540-604;
    Tr. by Peter J. Scagnelli, b.1949, ©
Tune: ERHALT UNS HERR, LM; Klug's *Geistliche Lieder,* 1543;
    Harm. by J. S. Bach, 1685-1750

All Creatures of Our God and King

1. All crea-tures of our God and King, Lift
2. O rush-ing wind and breez-es soft, O
3. O flow-ing wa-ters, pure and clear, Make
4. Dear moth-er earth, who day by day Un-
5. O ev-'ry one of ten-der heart, For-

up your voice and with us sing: Al-le-
clouds that ride the winds a - loft: Al-le-
mu-sic for your Lord to hear. Al-le-
folds rich bless-ings on our way, Al-le-
giv-ing oth-ers, take your part, Al-le-

lu - ia! Al-le-lu-ia! O
lu - ia! Al-le-lu-ia! O
lu - ia! Al-le-lu-ia! O
lu - ia! Al-le-lu-ia! The
lu - ia! Al-le-lu-ia! All

burn-ing sun with gold-en beam And
ris-ing morn, in praise re - joice, O
fire so mas-ter-ful and bright, Pro-
fruits and flow'rs that ver-dant grow, Let
you who pain and sor-row bear, Praise

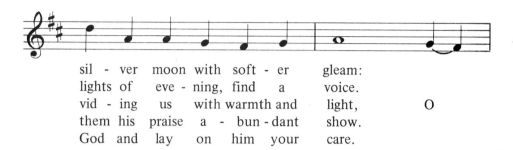

sil - ver moon with soft - er gleam:
lights of eve - ning, find a voice.
vid - ing us with warmth and light, O
them his praise a - bun - dant show.
God and lay on him your care.

praise God! O praise God! Al- le - lu - ia, al - le-

lu - ia, al - le - lu - ia!

6. And you, most kind and gentle death,
Waiting to hush our final breath,
Alleluia! Alleluia!
You lead to heav'n the child of God,
And Christ our Lord the way has trod.
O praise God! O praise God!
Alleluia, alleluia, alleluia!

7. Let all things their Creator bless,
And worship him in humbleness,
Alleluia! Alleluia!
O praise the Father, praise the Son,
And praise the Spirit, Three in One!
O praise God! O praise God!
Alleluia, alleluia, alleluia!

Text: *Laudato si, mi Signor;* Francis of Assisi, 1182-1226;
   Tr. by William H. Draper, 1855-1933, alt.
Tune: LASST UNS ERFREUEN, LM with alleluias; *Geistliche Kirchengesänge,* 1623;
   Harm. by Ralph Vaughan Williams, 1872-1958, © Oxford University Press

All Hail the Power of Jesus' Name

1. All hail the pow'r of Je - sus' name! Let
2. Crown him, ye mar - tyrs of our God, Who
3. O that, with yon - der sa - cred throng, We

an - gels pros - trate fall; Bring
from his al - tar call; Ex-
at his feet may fall, Join

forth the roy - al di - a-dem, And crown him Lord of
tol the stem of Jes - se's rod, And crown him Lord of
in the ev - er - last - ing song, And crown him Lord of

all, And crown him Lord of all, And
all, And crown him Lord of all, And
all, And crown him Lord of all, And

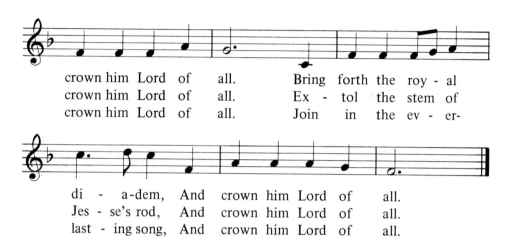

crown him Lord of all. Bring forth the roy - al
crown him Lord of all. Ex - tol the stem of
crown him Lord of all. Join in the ev - er-

di - a-dem, And crown him Lord of all.
Jes - se's rod, And crown him Lord of all.
last - ing song, And crown him Lord of all.

Text: Edward Perronet, 1726-1792; alt. by John Rippon, 1751-1836, alt.
Tune: DIADEM, CM with repeats; From the *Primitive Baptist Hymn and Tune Book,*
1902; Harm. by Richard Proulx, b.1937, © 1975, GIA Publications, Inc.

All Things Bright and Beautiful

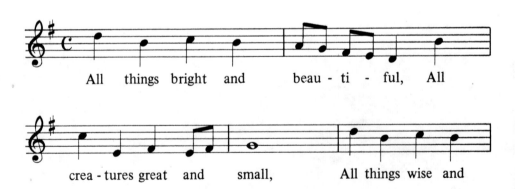

All things bright and beau - ti - ful, All
crea - tures great and small, All things wise and

won - der - ful, The Lord God made them all.

1. Each lit - tle flower that o - pens, Each
2. The pur - ple - head - ed moun - tain, The
3. The cold wind in the win - ter, The
4. God gave us eyes to see them, And

lit - tle bird that sings, God made their glow - ing
riv - er run - ning by, The sun - set, and the
pleas-ant sum - mer sun, The ripe fruits in the
lips that we might tell How great is God Al-

D.C.

col - ors, God made their ti - ny wings.
morn - ing That bright - ens up the sky.
gar - den, God made them ev - 'ry one.
might - y, Who has made all things well.

Text: Cecil F. Alexander, 1818-1895, alt.
Tune: ROYAL OAK, 7 6 7 6 with refrain; English Melody;
Adapted by Martin Shaw, 1875-1958

Alleluia, Sing to Jesus

1. Al - le - lu - ia! sing to Je - sus!
2. Al - le - lu - ia! not as or - phans
* 3. Al - le - lu - ia! Bread of An - gels,
* 4. Al - le - lu - ia! King e - ter - nal,

His the scep - ter, his the throne;
Are we left in sor - row now;
Here on earth our food, our stay!
You the Lord of lords we own;

Al - le - lu - ia! his the tri - umph,
Al - le - lu - ia! he is near us,
Al - le - lu - ia! here the sin - ful
Al - le - lu - ia! born of Mar - y,

His the vic - to - ry a - lone;
Faith be - lieves, nor ques - tions how:
Flee to you from day to day:
Earth your foot - stool, heav'n your throne:

Hark! the songs of peace - ful Zi - on
Though the cloud from sight re - ceived him,
In - ter - ces - sor, friend of sin - ners,
You with - in the veil have en - tered,

Thun - der like a might - y flood;
When the for - ty days were o'er,
Earth's re - deem - er, plead for me,
Robed in flesh, our great high priest;

Je - sus out of ev - 'ry na - tion
Shall our hearts for - get his prom - ise,
Where the songs of all the sin - less
Here on earth both priest and vic - tim

Has re - deemed us by his blood.
"I am with you ev - er - more"?
Sweep a - cross the crys - tal sea.
In the eu - cha - ris - tic feast.

* Optional

Text: Rev. 5-9; William C. Dix, 1837-1898
Tune: HYFRYDOL, 8 7 8 7 D; Rowland H. Prichard, 1811-1887

Amazing Grace

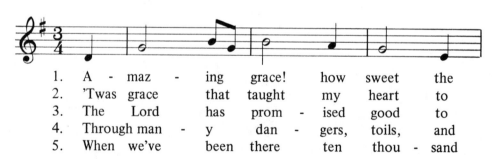

1.	A - maz	- ing	grace!	how	sweet	the
2.	'Twas grace	that	taught	my	heart	to
3.	The Lord	has	prom - ised	good	to
4.	Through man - y	dan - gers,	toils,	and
5.	When we've	been	there	ten	thou - sand

sound,   That   saved   a   wretch   like   me!
fear,   And   grace   my   fears   re - lieved;
me,   His   word   my   hope   se - cures;
snares,   I   have   al - read - y   come;
years,   Bright shin - ing   as   the   sun,

I   once   was   lost,   but   now   am
How   pre - cious   did   that   grace   ap-
He   will   my   shield   and   por - tion
'Tis   grace   has   brought   me   safe   thus
We've   no   less   days   to   sing   God's

found,   Was   blind,   but   now   I   see.
pear   The   hour   I   first   be - lieved!
be   As   long   as   life   en - dures.
far,   And   grace   will   lead   me   home.
praise   Than   when   we'd   first   be - gun.

Text: St. 1-4, John Newton, 1725-1807; St. 5, Ascr. to John Rees, fl.1859
Tune: NEW BRITAIN, CM; *Virginia Harmony;* 1831; Harm. by John Barnard, b.1948,
    © 1982, Hope Publishing Co.

Blessed Feasts of Blessed Martyrs

1. Bless - ed feasts of bless - ed mar - tyrs,
2. Faith pre - vail - ing, hope un - fail - ing,
3. There - fore, all that reign in glo - ry,

Ho - ly wom - en, ho - ly men, With our love and
Lov - ing Christ with sin - gle heart, Thus they, glo - rious
Strong and sure with Christ on high, Join to ours your

ad - mi - ra - tion, Greet we your re - turn a - gain.
and vic - to - rious, Brave - ly bore the mar - tyr's part,
sup - pli - ca - tion When be - fore him we draw nigh,

Wor - thy deeds are theirs, and won - ders,
By con - tempt of ev - 'ry an - guish,
Pray - ing that, this life com - plet - ed,

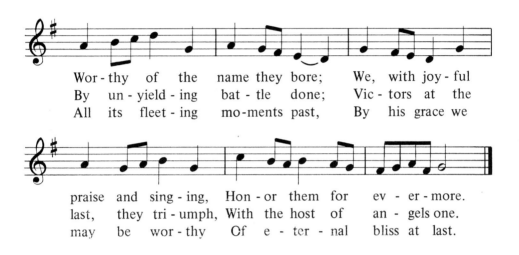

Wor - thy of the name they bore; We, with joy - ful
By un - yield - ing bat - tle done; Vic - tors at the
All its fleet - ing mo - ments past, By his grace we

praise and sing - ing, Hon - or them for ev - er - more.
last, they tri - umph, With the host of an - gels one.
may be wor - thy Of e - ter - nal bliss at last.

Text: *O beata beatorum;* Latin, 12th C.; Tr. by John M. Neale, 1818-1866, alt.
Tune: IN BABILONE, 8 7 8 7 D; *Oude en Nieuwe Hollanste Boerenlities,* c.1710

Blest Are They

1. Blest are they, the poor in spir-it, theirs is the

king-dom of God. Blest are they,

full of sor-row, they shall be con - soled.

Refrain

Re - joice and be glad! Bless - ed are

you, ho - ly are you! Re - joice and be

glad! Yours is the king-dom of God!

2. Blest are they, the low - ly ones, they shall in-
3. Blest are they who show mer - cy, mer - cy

her - it the earth.   Blest are they who
shall be theirs.   Blest are they, the

D.S.

hun-ger and thirst,   they shall have their fill.
pure of heart,   they shall see God!

4. Blest are they who seek peace;
5. Blest are you who suf - fer hate,

they are the chil - dren of God.
all be - cause of me. Re-

Blest are they who suf - fer in faith, the
joice and be glad, yours is the king-dom;

D.S.

glo - ry of God is theirs.
shine for all to see.

Text: Matthew 5:3-12; David Haas, b.1957
Tune: David Haas, b.1957; Vocal arr. by David Haas, b.1957, Michael Joncas, b.1951
© 1985, GIA Publications, Inc.

113

Bring Forth the Kingdom

Verses

Cantor:

1. You are salt for the earth, O peo-ple:
2. You are a light on the hill, O peo-ple:
3. You are a seed of the Word, O peo-ple:
4. We are a blest and a pil - grim peo-ple:

All:

Salt for the King-dom of God!
Light for the Cit - y of God!
Bring forth the King-dom of God!
Bound for the King-dom of God!

Cantor:

Share the fla - vor of life, O peo - ple:
Shine so ho - ly and bright, O peo - ple:
Seeds of mer-cy and seeds of jus - tice,
Love our jour-ney and love our home - land:

All:

Life in the King-dom of God!
Shine for the King-dom of God!
Grow in the King-dom of God!
Love is the King-dom of God!

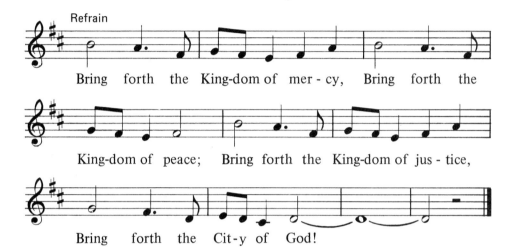

Bring forth the King-dom of mer - cy, Bring forth the

King-dom of peace; Bring forth the King-dom of jus - tice,

Bring forth the Cit-y of God!

Text: Matthew 5:13-15; Marty Haugen, b.1950
Tune: Marty Haugen, b.1950
© 1986, GIA Publications, Inc.

Come, Ye Thankful People, Come

1. Come, ye thank - ful peo - ple, come,
2. All the world is God's own field,
3. For the Lord our God shall come,
4. E - ven so, Lord, quick - ly come

Raise the song of har-vest-home: All is safe - ly
Fruit un- to God's praise to yield; Wheat and tares to-
And shall take the har-vest home; From his field shall
To your fi - nal har-vest home; Gath - er all your

gath - ered in, Ere the win - ter storms be - gin;
geth - er sown, Un - to joy or sor - row grown;
in that day All of - fens - es purge a - way;
peo - ple in, Free from sor - row, free from sin;

God, our Mak - er, does pro - vide
First the blade, and then the ear,
Give the an - gels charge at last
There, for ev - er pu - ri - fied,

For our wants to be sup-plied; Come to God's own
Then the full corn shall ap-pear: Grant, O har - vest
In the fire the tares to cast, But the fruit - ful
In your pres-ence to a - bide: Come, with all your

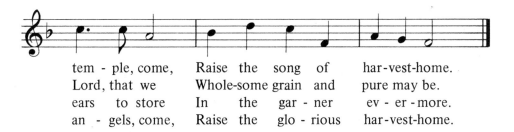

tem - ple, come,   Raise the song of   har-vest-home.
Lord, that we   Whole-some grain and   pure may be.
ears to store   In the gar - ner   ev - er - more.
an - gels, come,   Raise the glo - rious   har-vest-home.

Text: Henry Alford, 1810-1871, alt.
Tune: ST. GEORGE'S WINDSOR, 77 77 D; George J. Elvey, 1816-1893

Earth and All Stars

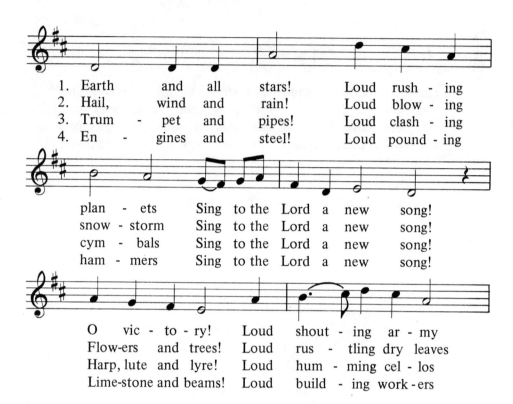

1. Earth and all stars! Loud rush - ing
2. Hail, wind and rain! Loud blow - ing
3. Trum - pet and pipes! Loud clash - ing
4. En - gines and steel! Loud pound - ing

plan - ets Sing to the Lord a new song!
snow - storm Sing to the Lord a new song!
cym - bals Sing to the Lord a new song!
ham - mers Sing to the Lord a new song!

O vic - to - ry! Loud shout - ing ar - my
Flow-ers and trees! Loud rus - tling dry leaves
Harp, lute and lyre! Loud hum - ming cel - los
Lime-stone and beams! Loud build - ing work - ers

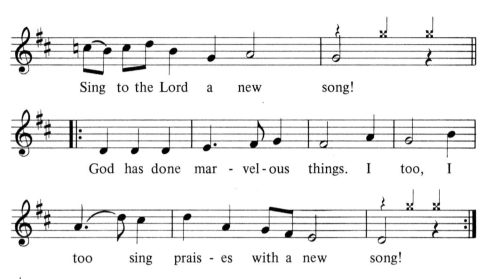

Sing to the Lord a new song!

God has done mar - vel - ous things. I too, I

too sing prais - es with a new song!

♩ *indicates clapping of hands*

5. Classrooms and labs! Loud boiling test tubes
    Sing to the Lord a new song!
   Athlete and band! Loud cheering people
    Sing to the Lord a new song!

6. Knowledge and truth! Loud sounding wisdom
    Sing to the Lord a new song!
   Daughter and son! Loud praying members
    Sing to the Lord a new song!

Text: Herbert Brokering, b.1926
Tune: EARTH AND ALL STARS, 4 5 7 D with refrain; Jan Bender, b.1909
© 1968, Augsburg Publishing House

Eat This Bread

Eat this bread, drink this cup, come to me and

nev-er be hun - gry. Eat this bread,

drink this cup, trust in me and you will not thirst.

Text: John 6; Adapted by Robert J. Batastini, b.1942 and the Taizé Community, 1984
Tune: Jacques Berthier, b.1923
© 1984, Les Presses de Taizé

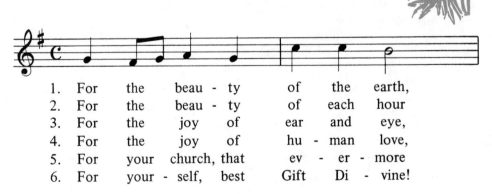

For the Beauty of the Earth

1. For	the	beau - ty	of	the	earth,
2. For	the	beau - ty	of	each	hour
3. For	the	joy	of	ear	and	eye,
4. For	the	joy	of	hu - man	love,
5. For	your	church, that	ev - er - more
6. For	your - self,	best	Gift	Di - vine!

For the glo - ry of the skies,
Of the day and of the night,
For the heart and mind's de - light,
Broth - er, sis - ter, par - ent, child,
Lifts its ho - ly hands a - bove,
To this world so free - ly given;

For the love which from our birth
Hill and vale, and tree and flower,
For the mys - tic har - mo - ny
Friends on earth, and friends a - bove;
Of - fering up on ev - 'ry shore
Word In - car - nate, God's de - sign,

O - ver and a - round us lies:
Sun and moon, and stars of light:
Link - ing sense to sound and sight:
For all gen - tle thoughts and mild:
Its pure sac - ri - fice of love:
Peace on earth and joy in heaven:

Lord of all, to you we raise This our hymn of grate - ful praise.

Text: Folliot S. Pierpont, 1835-1917, alt.
Tune: DIX, 77 77 77; Arr. from Conrad Kocher, 1786-1872,
    by William H. Monk, 1823-1889

Freedom Is Coming

O yes, I know, O yes, I

yes, I know.

O Jesus, O Jesus,
O Jesus, Jesus is coming,
O yes, I know,

Text: South African
Tune: South African
© 1984, Utryck

Gather Us In

1. Here in this place,   new light is stream-ing,
2. We are the young— our   lives are a mys-t'ry,
3. Here we will take the   wine and the wa-ter,
4. Not in the dark of   build-ings con-fin-ing,

Now is the dark - ness van-ished a-way,
We are the old who yearn for your face,
Here we will take the bread of new birth,
Not in some heav - en, light years a-way, But

See, in this space, our fears and our dream-ings,
We have been sung through-out all of his-t'ry,
Here you shall call your sons and your daugh-ters,
here in this place, the new light is shin-ing,

Brought here to you in the light of this
Called to be light to the whole hu-man
Call us a-new to be salt for the
Now is the King-dom, now is the

day.   Gath-er us in— the
race.   Gath-er us in— the
earth.   Give us to drink the
day.   Gath-er us in and

124

lost and for - sak - en,   Gath - er us in—   the
rich and the haugh - ty,   Gath - er us in—   the
wine of com - pas - sion,   Give us to eat   the
hold us for ev - er,   Gath - er us in   and

blind and the lame;   Call to us now,   and
proud and the strong;   Give us a heart   so
bread that is you;   Nour - ish us well, and
make us your own;   Gath - er us in—   all

we shall a - wak - en,   We shall a - rise at the
meek and so low - ly,   Give us the cour - age to
teach us to fash - ion   Lives that are ho - ly and
peo - ples to - geth - er, Fire of love in our

sound of our   name.
en - ter the   song.
hearts that are   true.
flesh and our   bone.

Gift of Finest Wheat

You sat-is-fy the hun-gry heart With

gift of fin-est wheat; Come give to us, O

sav-ing Lord, The bread of life to eat.

1. As when the shep - herd calls his sheep, They
2. With joy - ful lips we sing to you Our
3. Is not the cup we bless and share The
4. The mys - t'ry of your pres-ence, Lord, No
5. You give your - self to us, O Lord; Then

know and heed his voice; So when you call your
praise and grat - i - tude, That you should count us
blood of Christ out-poured? Do not one cup, one
mor - tal tongue can tell: Whom all the world can-
self - less let us be, To serve each oth - er

126

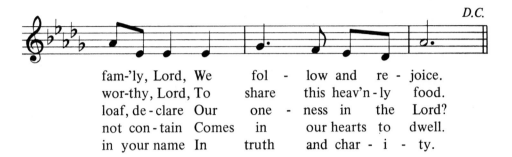

fam-'ly, Lord, We   fol - low and re - joice.
wor-thy, Lord, To   share this heav'n - ly food.
loaf, de - clare Our   one - ness in the Lord?
not con - tain Comes in   our hearts to dwell.
in your name In   truth and char - i - ty.

Text: Omer Westendorf, b.1916
Tune: BICENTENNIAL, CM with refrain; Robert E. Kreutz, b.1922

Gloria, Gloria

Canon

Glo - ri - a, glo - ri - a, in ex - cel - sis De - o!

Glo - ri - a, glo - ri - a, al - le - lu - ia, al - le - lu - ia!

Text: Luke 2:14; Taizé Community, 1978
Tune: Jacques Berthier, b.1923
© 1979, Les Presses de Taizé

Go Tell It on the Mountain

Go tell it on the moun - tain,

O - ver the hills and ev - 'ry - where; Go tell it on the

moun - tain That Je - sus Christ is born!

1. While shep - herds kept their watch - ing O'er
2. The shep - herds feared and trem - bled When
3. Down in a low - ly man - ger The

si - lent flocks by night, Be - hold through - out the
lo! a - bove the earth Rang out the an - gel
hum - ble Christ was born, And God sent us sal-

D.C.

heav - ens There shone a ho - ly light.
cho - rus That hailed our Sav - ior's birth.
va - tion That bless - ed Christ - mas morn.

Text: Afro-American Spiritual; Adapt. by John W. Work, Jr., 1871-1925
© Mrs. John W. Work III
Tune: GO TELL IT ON THE MOUNTAIN, 7 6 7 6 with refrain; Afro-American Spiritual;
Harm. by Paul Sjolund, b.1935, © Walton Music Corp.

129

God, Who Stretched the Spangled Heavens

1. God, who stretched the span - gled heav - ens
2. Proud - ly rise our mod - ern cit - ies,
3. We have ven - tured worlds un - dreamed of
4. As each far ho - ri - zon beck - ons,

In - fi - nite in time and place,
State - ly build - ings, row on row;
Since the child - hood of our race;
May it chal - lenge us a - new,

Flung the suns in burn - ing ra - diance
Yet their win - dows, blank, un - feel - ing,
Known the ec - sta - sy of wing - ing
Chil - dren of cre - a - tive pur - pose,

Through the si - lent fields of space;
Stare on can - yoned streets be - low,
Through un - trav - eled realms of space;
Serv - ing oth - ers, hon - oring you.

We, your chil - dren, in your like - ness,
Where the lone - ly drift un - no - ticed
Probed the se - crets of the at - om,
May our dreams prove rich with prom - ise,

Share in - ven - tive pow'rs with you;
In the cit - y's ebb and flow,
Yield - ing un - i - mag - ined power,
Each en - deav - or, well be - gun:

Great Cre - a - tor, still cre - at - ing,
Lost to pur - pose and to mean - ing,
Fac - ing us with life's de - struc - tion
Great Cre - a - tor, give us guid - ance

Show us what we yet may do.
Scarce - ly car - ing where they go.
Or our most tri - um - phant hour.
Till our goals and yours are one.

Text: Catherine Cameron, b.1927, © 1967, Hope Publishing Co.
Tune: HOLY MANNA, 8 7 8 7 D; William Moore, fl.1830; Harm. by Charles Anders, b.1929
   © 1969, Contemporary Worship I: Hymns

Holy, Holy, Holy! Lord God Almighty

1. Ho - ly, Ho - ly, Ho - ly! Lord God Al-
2. Ho - ly, Ho - ly, Ho - ly! all the saints a-
* 3. Ho - ly, Ho - ly, Ho - ly! though the dark - ness
4. Ho - ly, Ho - ly, Ho - ly! Lord God Al-

might - y! Ear - ly in the morn - ing our
dore thee, Cast - ing down their gold - en crowns a-
hide thee, Though the eye made blind by sin thy
might - y! All thy works shall praise thy Name in

song shall rise to thee: Ho - ly, Ho - ly,
round the glass - y sea; Cher - u - bim and
glo - ry may not see, On - ly thou art
earth, and sky, and sea; Ho - ly, Ho - ly,

Ho - ly! mer - ci - ful and might - y,
ser - a - phim fall - ing down be - fore thee,
ho - ly; there is none be - side thee,
Ho - ly! mer - ci - ful and might - y,

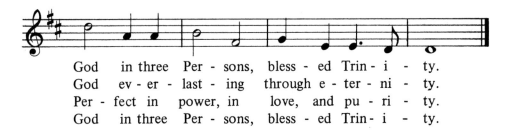

God in three Per - sons, bless - ed Trin - i - ty.
God ev - er - last - ing through e - ter - ni - ty.
Per - fect in power, in love, and pu - ri - ty.
God in three Per - sons, bless - ed Trin - i - ty.

*Optional

Text: Reginald Heber, 1783-1826, alt.
Tune: NICAEA, 11 12 12 10; John B. Dykes, 1823-1876

I Am the Bread of Life

1. ___ I am the Bread of life. You who
2. The bread that__ I will give is my
3. Un - less___ you___ eat of the
4. ___ I am the Res - ur - rec - tion,___
5. Yes, Lord,___ I be - lieve___ that ___

come to me shall not hun - ger; and who be-
flesh for the life of the world,___ and if you
flesh of the Son of Man___ and ___
I___ am the life.___ If you be-
you___ are the Christ,___ the ___

lieve in me shall not thirst. No one can come to
eat___ of this bread, you shall live for
drink___ of his blood, and drink___ of his
lieve___ in ___ me, e - ven though you
Son ___ of ___ God, Who___ have ___

me un - less the Fa - ther beck - ons.
ev - er, you shall live for ev - er.
blood, you shall not have life with - in you.
die,___ you shall live for ev - er.
come in - to___ the___ world.___

And I will raise you up, and I will

raise you up, and I will raise you

up on the last day.

Text: John 6; Suzanne Toolan, SM, b.1927
Tune: BREAD OF LIFE, Irregular with refrain; Suzanne Toolan, b.1927
© 1970, GIA Publications, Inc.

I Received the Living God

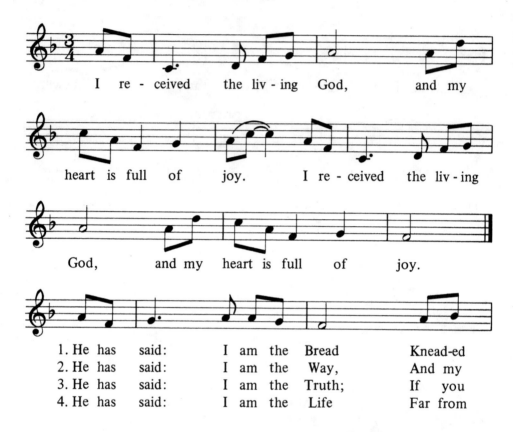

I re - ceived the liv - ing God, and my

heart is full of joy. I re - ceived the liv - ing

God, and my heart is full of joy.

1. He has said: I am the Bread Knead-ed
2. He has said: I am the Way, And my
3. He has said: I am the Truth; If you
4. He has said: I am the Life Far from

long to give you   life;   You who will   par-take of
Fa - ther longs for   you;   So I   come   to bring you
fol - low close   to   me,   You will know   me in your
whom no thing can   grow,   But re - ceive   this liv - ing

D.C.

me   Need not   ev - er   fear   to   die.
home   To   be   one with God   a -   new.
heart,   And my   word shall make you   free.
bread,   And my   Spir - it   you   shall   know.

Text: Anonymous
Tune: LIVING GOD, 7 7 7 7 with refrain; Anonymous; Harm. by Richard Proulx, b.1937
    © 1986, GIA Publications, Inc.

I Want to Walk as a Child of the Light

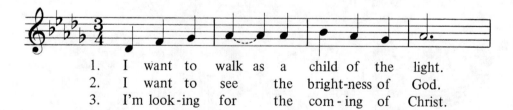

1. I want to walk as a child of the light.
2. I want to see the bright-ness of God.
3. I'm look-ing for the com-ing of Christ.

I want to fol - low Je - sus.
I want to look at Je - sus.
I want to be with Je - sus.

God set the stars to give light to the world. The
Clear sun of right-eous-ness shine on my path, And
When we have run with pa - tience the race, We

star of my life is Je - sus.
show me the way to the Fa - ther.
shall know the joy of Je - sus.

In him there is no dark - ness at all. The

night and the day are both a - like. The

Lamb is the light of the cit - y of God.

Shine in my heart, Lord Je - sus.

Text: Eph. 5:8-10; Rev. 21:23; Jn. 12:46; I Jn. 1:5; Heb. 12:1; Kathleen Thomerson, b.1934
Tune: HOUSTON, 10 7 10 8 9 9 10 7; Kathleen Thomerson, b.1934
© 1970, 1975, Celebration

Immaculate Mary

1. Im - ma - cu - late Mar - y, your
2. Pre - des - tined for Christ by e-
3. To you by an an - gel, the
4. Most blest of all wom - en, you
5. The an - gels re - joiced when you

prais - es we sing; You reign now in
ter - nal de - cree, God willed you both
Lord God made known The grace of the
heard and be - lieved, Most blest in the
brought forth God's Son; Your joy is the

splen - dor with Je - sus our King.
vir - gin and moth - er to be.
Spir - it, the gift of the Son.
fruit of your womb then con - ceived.
joy of all a - ges to come.

A - ve, A - ve, A - ve, Ma - ri - a.

A - ve, A - ve, Ma - ri - a.

6. Your child is the Savior, all hope lies in him:
   He gives us new life and redeems us from sin.

7. In glory for ever now close to your Son,
   All ages will praise you for all God has done.

Text: St. 1, Jeremiah Cummings, 1814-1866, alt.; St. 2-7, Brian Foley, b.1919
© 1971, Faber Music Ltd.
Tune: LOURDES HYMN, 11 11 with refrain; Grenoble, 1882

In Christ There Is No East or West

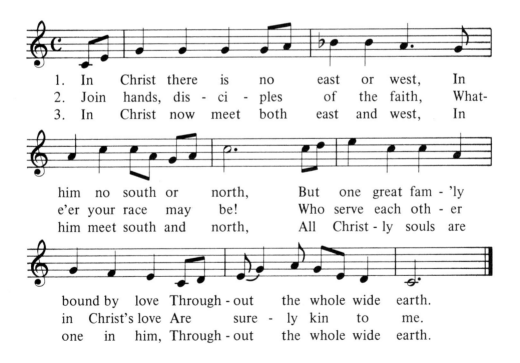

1. In Christ there is no east or west, In
2. Join hands, dis - ci - ples of the faith, What-
3. In Christ now meet both east and west, In

him no south or north, But one great fam - 'ly
e'er your race may be! Who serve each oth - er
him meet south and north, All Christ - ly souls are

bound by love Through - out the whole wide earth.
in Christ's love Are sure - ly kin to me.
one in him, Through - out the whole wide earth.

Text: Gal. 3:28; John Oxenham, 1852-1941, © American Tract Society
Tune: MC KEE, CM; Afro-American; Adapted by Harry T. Burleigh, 1866-1949

In the Lord I'll Be Ever Thankful

In the Lord I'll be ev-er thank-ful, in the
Lord I will re-joice! Look to him, do not be a-
fraid; in him re-joic - ing: the Lord is
near, in him re-joic - ing: the Lord is near.

Text: Taizé Community
Tune: Jacques Berthier, b.1923
© 1986, Les Presses de Taizé

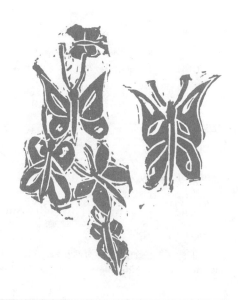

Jesu, Jesu, Fill Us with Your Love

Je - su, Je - su, fill us with your love, show

us how to serve the neigh-bors we have from you.

1. Kneels at the feet of his friends, Si - lent-ly wash-es their
2. Neigh-bors are rich and poor, Neigh-bors are black and
3. These are the ones we should serve, These are the ones we should
4. Kneel at the feet of our friends, Si - lent-ly wash-ing their

D.C.

feet, Mas - ter who pours out him - self for them.
white, Neigh-bors are near and far a - way.
love. All are neigh-bors to us and you.
feet, This is the way we should live with you.

Text: John 13:3-5; Ghana Folk Song; Tr. by Tom Colvin, b.1925
Tune: CHEREPONI, Irregular; Ghana Folk Song; Acc. by Jane M. Marshall, b.1924
© 1969, 1982, Hope Publishing Co.

Jesus Christ Is Risen Today

1. Je - sus Christ is ris'n to - day, Al - le-
2. Hymns of praise then let us sing, Al - le-
3. But the pains which he en - dured, Al - le-
4. Sing we to our God a - bove, Al - le-

lu - ia! Our tri - um - phant ho - ly day,
lu - ia! Un - to Christ, our heav'n - ly King,
lu - ia! Our sal - va - tion have pro - cured;
lu - ia! Praise e - ter - nal for such love;

Al - le - lu - ia! Who did once up-
Al - le - lu - ia! Who en - dured the
Al - le - lu - ia! Now a - bove the
Al - le - lu - ia! Praise our God, let

on the cross, Al - le - lu - ia!
cross and grave, Al - le - lu - ia!
sky he's King, Al - le - lu - ia!
all con - fess, Al - le - lu - ia!

Suf - fer to re - deem our loss. Al - le - lu - ia!
Sin - ners to re - deem and save. Al - le - lu - ia!
Where the an - gels ev - er sing. Al - le - lu - ia!
Fa - ther, Son, and Spir - it blest. Al - le - lu - ia!

Text: St. 1, *Surrexit Christus hodie*, Latin, 14th C.; Para. in *Lyra Davidica*, 1708, alt.;
St. 2, 3, *The Compleat Psalmodist*, c.1750, alt.; St. 4, Charles Wesley, 1707-1788
Tune: EASTER HYMN, 77 77 with alleluias; *Lyra Davidica*, 1708

Jesus, Remember Me

Je - sus, re - mem - ber me
when you come in - to your King - dom. Je - sus, re-
mem - ber me when you come in - to your King - dom.

Text: Luke 23:42; Taizé Community, 1981
Tune: Jacques Berthier, b.1923
© 1981, Les Presses de Taizé

145

Joy to the World

1. Joy to the world! the Lord is come: Let
2. Joy to the world! the Sav - ior reigns: Let
3. He rules the world with truth and grace, And

earth re - ceive her King; Let ev - 'ry
us, our songs em - ploy; While fields and
makes the na - tions prove The glo - ries

heart pre - pare him room, And
floods, rocks, hills, and plains; Re-
of his right - eous - ness, And

heaven and na - ture sing, And
peat the sound - ing joy, Re-
won - ders of his love, And

heaven and na - ture sing, And
peat the sound - ing joy, Re-
won - ders of his love, And

heaven,	and	heaven	and	na - ture	sing.
peat,	re - peat	the	sound - ing	joy.
won - ders,	won - ders	of	his	love.

Text: Ps. 98; Isaac Watts, 1674-1748
Tune: ANTIOCH, CM; Arr. from George F. Handel, 1685-1759,
in T. Hawkes' *Collection of Tunes,* 1833

Jubilate Deo

Canon - *2 voices*

Ju- bi - la - te De-o om-nis ter - ra.

Ser -vi - te Do-mi-no in lae - ti - ti - a.

Al - le -lu - ia, al - le -lu - ia, in lae -ti - ti - a.

Al - le - lu -ia, al - le -lu - ia, in lae-ti - ti - a!

Text: Psalm 100, *Rejoice in God, all the earth. Serve the Lord with gladness;*
Taizé Community, 1978
Tune: Jacques Berthier, b.1923
© 1979, Les Presses de Taizé

Let All on Earth Their Voices Raise

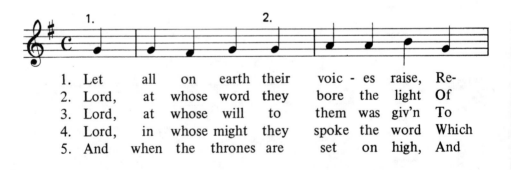

1. Let all on earth their voic - es raise, Re-
2. Lord, at whose word they bore the light Of
3. Lord, at whose will to them was giv'n To
4. Lord, in whose might they spoke the word Which
5. And when the thrones are set on high, And

sound - ing   heav - en's   joy - ful   praise   To
gos - pel   truth   to   dark - est   night,   To
bind   and   loose   in   earth   and   heav'n,   Our
cured   dis - ease   and   health   re - stored,   To
judg - ment's   awe - some   hour   draws   nigh,   Then,

God   who   gave the A - pos - tles   grace   To
us   that   heav'n - ly   light   im - part,   Make
chains   un - bind,   our   sins   un - do,   And
us   its   heal - ing   pow'r   pro - long,   Sup-
Lord,   with   them   pro - nounce   us   blest,   And

run   on   earth   their   glo - rious   race.
glad   our   eyes   and   cheer   our   heart.
in   our   hearts   your   grace   re - new.
port   the   weak,   con - firm   the   strong.
take   us   to   your   end - less   rest.

Text: *Exsultet orbis gaudiis;* Latin, 10th C.; Tr. by Richard Mant, 1776-1848, alt.
Tune: TALLIS' CANON, LM; Thomas Tallis, c.1505-1585

Let All Things Now Living

1. Let   all things now   liv - ing A   song   of   thanks - giv - ing
2. These laws God en - forc - es: The stars in   their cours - es,

To   God   our   Cre -   a - tor tri - um - phant - ly   raise;
The sun   in   its   or - bit o - be - dient - ly   shine,

Who fash - ioned and   made us, Pro - tect - ed   and   stayed us,
The hills and   the   moun-tains, The riv - ers and   foun - tains,

By   guid - ing us   on to the   end   of   our   days.
The depths of   the   o - cean pro - claim God di - vine.

God's ban - ners are   o'er us, Pure light goes be - fore us,
We,   too, should be   voic - ing Our love   and re - joic - ing

A   pil - lar   of   fire shin - ing forth in   the   night:
With glad ad - o -   ra - tion, a   song let us   raise:

Till   shad - ows have van - ished And dark - ness is   ban - ished,
Till   all things now   liv - ing U - nite in   thanks-giv - ing,

As for - ward we trav - el from light in - to Light.
To God in the high-est, ho - san - na and praise.

Text: Katherine K. Davis, 1892-1980, alt., © 1939, E.C. Schirmer Music Co.
Tune: ASH GROVE, 66 11 66 D; Welsh; Harm. by Gerald H. Knight, 1908-1979
    © The Royal School of Church Music

Let Us Break Bread Together

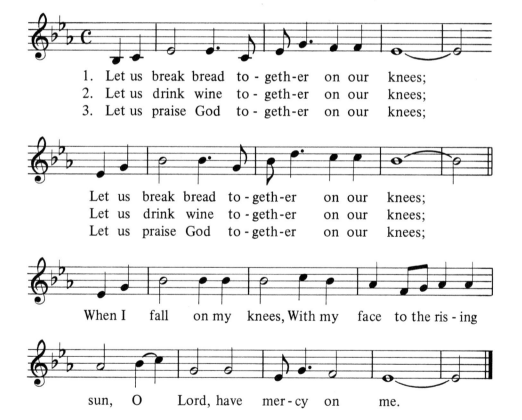

1. Let us break bread to - geth - er on our knees;
2. Let us drink wine to - geth-er on our knees;
3. Let us praise God to - geth-er on our knees;

Let us break bread to - geth-er on our knees;
Let us drink wine to - geth-er on our knees;
Let us praise God to - geth-er on our knees;

When I fall on my knees, With my face to the ris - ing

sun, O Lord, have mer - cy on me.

Text: American Folk Hymn
Tune: LET US BREAK BREAD, 10 10 6 8 7; American Folk Hymn;
    Harm. by David Hurd, b.1950, © 1986, GIA Publications, Inc.

Let Us Walk in the Light

1. Let us walk in the light of the
2. Let us live ev - 'ry day as our
3. Let us grow ev - er clos - er in
4. Let us bring forth your king - dom on
5. May we learn to be chil - dren a-

Lord, Let us sing of God's
last, Fill each one with our
love, Give us hearts o - ver-
earth, Show the spir - it of
gain, May each day bring us

love to all the earth. We are
laugh-ter and our tears. We are
flow - ing with your peace. We are
love to all we meet. We are
new dreams we can share. We are

still on our way, we are go - ing home to-

geth - er. Let us walk in the

152

light   of   the   Lord.

Text: Marty Haugen, b.1950
Tune: Marty Haugen, b.1950
© 1982, GIA Publications, Inc.

Let Us with Joy Our Voices Raise

1. Let   us   with joy our   voic - es raise   In
2. O   Strength of all the   strong, God's Son, Through
3. Praise God, Cre - a - tor, God the   Son,   And

that   he - ro - ic   wo - man's praise, Whose
whom a - lone great   deeds are   done,   By
God   the   Spir - it,   Three in   One,   Who

cour - age, strength and   ho - ly   fame   Have
your great strength and   through her   prayer May
gave this   no - ble   wo - man grace   A

giv - en   her   an   hon - ored name.
we   bear   wit - ness   ev - 'ry - where.
life   of   vir - tue   to   em - brace.

Text: *Fortem virili pectore;* Silvio Antoniano, 1540-1603; Tr. and St. 3 by
   Roger Nachtwey, b.1930, alt., © 1965, FEL Publications, Ltd.
Tune: EISENACH, LM; Johann H. Schein, 1586-1630; Harm. by J.S. Bach, 1685-1750

153

Lift High the Cross

Lift high the cross, the love of Christ pro - claim till

all the world a - dore his sa - cred name.

1. Come,   Chris - tians,   fol - low
2. Led   on   their way   by
3. Each   new - born fol - l'wer
4. O   Lord,   once lift - ed
5. So   shall   our song   of

where the Mas - ter trod,   our   King   vic-
this   tri - um - phant sign, the   hosts of
of   the Cru - ci - fied bears on   the
on   the glo - rious tree, your death has
tri - umph ev - er be: praise to   the

D.C.

to - rious,   Christ,   the Son of   God.
God   in   con - quering ranks com - bine.
brow the seal of   him who   died.
bought us   life e - ter - nal - ly.
Cru - ci - fied for vic - to - ry!

Text: 1 Cor. 1:18; George W. Kitchen, 1827-1912, and Michael R. Newbolt, 1874-1956, alt.
Tune: CRUCIFER, 10 10 with refrain; Sydney H. Nicholson, 1875-1947
© by permission of Hymns and Ancient and Modern, Ltd.

Lord of All Hopefulness

1. Lord of all hope - ful - ness, Lord of all
2. Lord of all ea - ger - ness, Lord of all
3. Lord of all kind - li - ness, Lord of all
4. Lord of all gen - tle - ness, Lord of all

joy, Whose trust, ev - er child - like, no
faith, Whose strong hands were skilled at the
grace, Your hands swift to wel - come, your
calm, Whose voice is con - tent - ment, whose

cares can de - stroy, Be there at our
plane and the lathe, Be there at our
arms to em - brace, Be there at our
pres - ence is balm, Be there at our

wak - ing, and give us, we pray, Your
la - bors, and give us, we pray, Your
hom - ing, and give us, we pray, Your
sleep - ing, and give us, we pray, Your

bliss in our hearts, Lord, at the break of the day.
strength in our hearts, Lord, at the noon of the day.
love in our hearts, Lord, at the eve of the day.
peace in our hearts, Lord, at the end of the day.

Text: Jan Struther, 1901-1953, © Oxford University Press
Tune: SLANE, 10 11 11 12; Gaelic; Harm. by Erik Routely, 1917-1982
    © 1985, Hope Publishing Co.

Lord, Who throughout These Forty Days

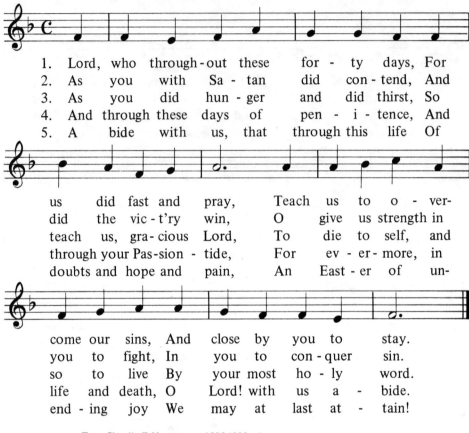

1. Lord, who through-out these for-ty days, For
2. As you with Sa-tan did con-tend, And
3. As you did hun-ger and did thirst, So
4. And through these days of pen-i-tence, And
5. A bide with us, that through this life Of

us did fast and pray, Teach us to o-ver-
did the vic-t'ry win, O give us strength in
teach us, gra-cious Lord, To die to self, and
through your Pas-sion - tide, For ev-er-more, in
doubts and hope and pain, An East-er of un-

come our sins, And close by you to stay.
you to fight, In you to con-quer sin.
so to live By your most ho-ly word.
life and death, O Lord! with us a - bide.
end-ing joy We may at last at - tain!

Text: Claudia F. Hernaman, 1838-1898, alt.
Tune: ST. FLAVIAN, CM; *John's Day Psalter*, 1562;
Harm. based on the original *faux-bourdon* setting

Lord, You Give the Great Commission

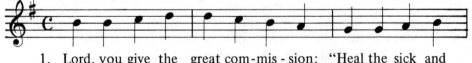

1. Lord, you give the great com-mis - sion: "Heal the sick and
2. Lord, you call us to your ser - vice: "In my name bap-
3. Lord, you make the com-mon ho - ly: "This my bod - y,
4. Lord, you show us love's true meas-ure: "Fa - ther, what they
5. Lord, you bless with words as-sur - ing: "I am with you

preach the word." Lest the Church ne - glect its mis - sion,
tize and teach." That the world may trust your prom - ise,
this my blood." Let us all, for earth's true glo - ry,
do, for-give." Yet we hoard as pri - vate treas - ure
to the end." Faith and hope and love re - stor - ing,

And the Gos - pel go un-heard, Help us wit - ness
Life a - bun-dant meant for each, Give us all that
Dai - ly lift life heav - en-ward, Ask - ing that the
All that you so free - ly give. May your care and
May we serve as you in - tend, And, a - mid the

to your pur - pose With re-newed in - teg - ri - ty;
fer - vor, draw us Clos - er in com - mun - i - ty;
world a - round us Share your chil-dren's lib - er - ty;
mer - cy lead us To a just so - ci - e - ty;
cares that claim us, Hold in mind e - ter - ni - ty;

With the Spir-it's gifts em-power us For the work of min - is-try.

Text: Jeffrey Rowthorn, b.1934, © 1978, Hope Publishing Co.
Tune: HYMN TO JOY, 8 7 8 7 D; Arr. from Ludwig van Beethoven, 1770-1827,
    by Edward Hodges, 1796-1867

Magnificat

Canon

Ma - gni-fi - cat,   ma - gni-fi - cat,   Ma - gni - fi - cat a - ni - ma

me - a   Do - mi - num. Ma - gni - fi - cat,   ma - gni - fi - cat,

Ma - gni - fi - cat a - ni - ma   me -   a!

Text: Luke 1:46, *My soul magnifies the Lord;* Taizé Community, 1978
Tune: Jacques Berthier, b.1923
© 1979, Les Presses de Taizé

Now Thank We All Our God

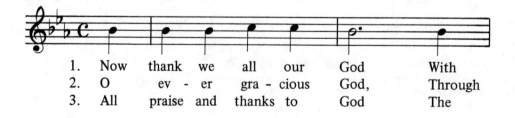

1. Now	thank	we	all	our	God	With
2. O	ev - er	gra - cious	God,			Through
3. All	praise	and	thanks	to	God	The

hearts and hands and voic - es, Who
all our life be near us, With
Fa - ther now be giv - en, The

won-drous things has done, In whom this world re-
ev - er joy - ful hearts And bless - ed peace to
Son, and Spir - it blest, Who reigns in high - est

joic - es; Who, from our moth-ers' arms, Has
cheer us; Pre - serve us in your grace, And
heav - en; E - ter - nal, Tri - une God, Whom

blessed us on our way With count - less gifts of
guide us in dis - tress, And free us from all
earth and heav'n a - dore; For thus it was, is

love, And still is ours to - day.
sin, Till heav - en we pos - sess.
now, And shall be ev - er - more.

Text: *Nun danket alle Gott;* Martin Rinkart, 1586-1649;
  Tr. by Catherine Winkworth, 1827-1878, alt.
Tune: NUN DANKET, 6 7 6 7 6 6 6 6; Johann Crüger, 1598-1662;
  Harm. by A. Gregory Murray, OSB, b.1905

Now We Remain

Refrain

We hold the death of the Lord deep in our hearts. Liv - ing; now we re-main with Je - sus the Christ.

Verses

1. Once we were peo ple a - fraid, lost in the
2. Some-thing which we have known, some-thing we've
3. He chose to give of him - self, be - came our
4. We are the pres - ence of God; this is our

night. Then by your cross we were saved;
touched, what we have seen with our eyes:
bread. Bro - ken, that we might live.
call. Now to be - come bread and wine:

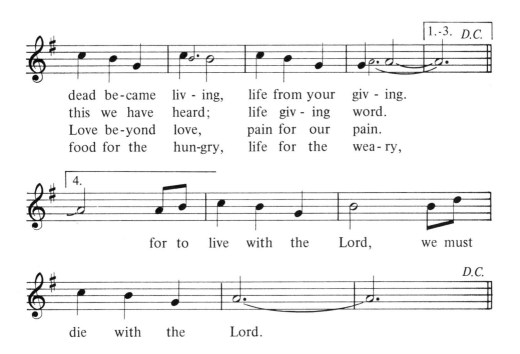

dead be-came liv - ing, life from your giv - ing.
this we have heard; life giv - ing word.
Love be-yond love, pain for our pain.
food for the hun-gry, life for the wea-ry,

for to live with the Lord, we must

die with the Lord.

Text: Corinthians, 1 John, 2 Timothy; David Haas, b.1957
Tune: David Haas, b.1957
© 1983, GIA Publications, Inc.

O Breathe on Me, O Breath of God

1. O breathe on me, O breath of God, Fill
2. O breathe on me, O breath of God, Un-
3. O breathe on me, O breath of God, My
4. O breathe on me, O breath of God: So

me with life a - new, That
til my heart is pure; Un-
will to yours in - cline, Un-
shall I nev - er die, But

I may love the things you love, And
til my will is one with yours, To
til this self - ish part of me Glows
live with you the per - fect life Of

162

do   what   you   would   do.
do   and   to   en - dure.
with   your   fire   di - vine.
your   e - ter - ni - ty.

Text: Edwin Hatch, 1835-1889
Tune: ST. COLUMBA, CM; Gaelic; Harm. by A. Gregory Murray, OSB, b.1905, ©

O Come, All Ye Faithful/Adeste Fideles

1. O come, all ye faith - ful, joy - ful and tri-
2. Sing, choirs of an - gels, sing in ex - ul-
3. Yea, Lord, we greet thee, born this hap - py
4. *Ad - é - ste fi - dé - les, laé - ti, tri - um-*

um - phant, O come ye, O come ye to
ta - tion, Sing, all ye cit - i - zens of
morn - ing, Je - sus, to thee be all
phán - tes, Ve - ní - te, ve - ní - te in

Beth - le - hem; Come and be-
heav'n a - bove! Glo - ry to
glo - ry giv'n; Word of the
Béth - le - hem. Na - tum vi-

hold him, born the King of an - gels;
God, all glo - ry in the high - est;
Fa - ther, now in flesh ap - pear - ing;
dé - te, Re - gem an - ge - ló - rum.

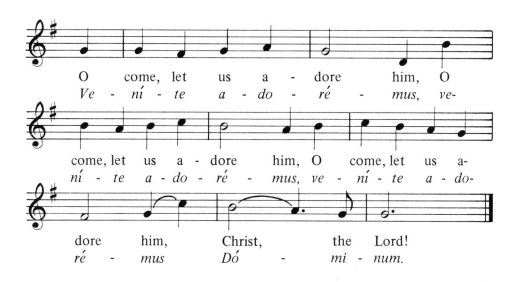

O come, let us a - dore him, O
Ve - ní - te a - do - ré - mus, ve-

come, let us a - dore him, O come, let us a-
ní - te a - do - ré - mus, ve - ní - te a - do-

dore him, Christ, the Lord!
ré - mus Dó - mi - num.

Text: *Adeste fideles;* John F. Wade, c.1711-1786; Tr. by Frederick Oakeley, 1802-1880, alt.
Tune: ADESTE FIDELES, Irr. with refrain; John F. Wade, c.1711-1786

O Come, O Come, Emmanuel

1. O come, O come, Em - man - u - el,
2. O come, O Wis - dom from on high,
3. O come, O come, great Lord of might,
4. O come, O Rod of Jes - se's stem,
5. O come, O Key of Dav - id, come,

And ran - som cap - tive Is - ra - el,
Who or - ders all things might - i - ly;
Who to your tribes on Si - nai's height
From ev - 'ry foe de - liv - er them
And o - pen wide our heav'n - ly home;

That mourns in lone - ly ex - ile here
To us the path of knowl - edge show,
In an - cient times once gave the law,
That trust your might - y pow'r to save,
Make safe the way that leads on high,

Un - til the Son of God ap - pear.
And teach us in her ways to go.
In cloud, and maj - es - ty, and awe.
And give them vic - t'ry o'er the grave.
And close the path to mis - er - y.

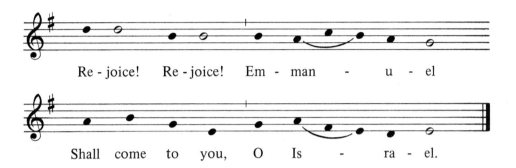

Re - joice! Re - joice! Em - man - u - el

Shall come to you, O Is - ra - el.

6. O come, O Dayspring from on high
   And cheer us by your drawing nigh;
   Disperse the gloomy clouds of night,
   And death's dark shadow put to flight.

7. O come, Desire of nations, bind
   In one the hearts of humankind;
   O bid our sad divisions cease,
   And be for us our King of Peace.

Text: *Veni, veni Emmanuel;* Latin 9th C.; Tr. by John M. Neale, 1818-1866, alt.
Tune: VENI, VENI EMMANUEL, LM with refrain; Mode I;
      Adapt. by Thomas Helmore, 1811-1890; Acc. by Richard Proulx, b.1937
      © 1975, GIA Publications, Inc.

O God of Love, O King of Peace

1. O God of love, O King of peace, Make
2. Whom shall we trust but you, O Lord? Where
3. Where saints and an - gels dwell a - bove, All

wars through - out the world to cease; Our
rest but on your faith - ful word? None
hearts are joined in ho - ly love; O

vio - lent ways help us con - tain; Give
ev - er called on you in vain; Give
bind us in that heav'n - ly chain; Give

peace, O God, give peace a - gain!
peace, O God, give peace a - gain!
peace, O God, give peace a - gain!

Text: Henry W. Baker, 1821-1877
Tune: TALLIS' CANON, LM; Thomas Tallis, d.1585

O Holy Spirit, by Whose Breath

1. O Ho-ly Spir-it, by whose breath
2. You are the seek-er's sure re - source,
3. In you God's en - er - gy is shown,
4. Flood our dull sens - es with your light;

Life ris - es vib - rant out of death:
Of burn-ing love the liv - ing source,
To us your var - ied gifts made known.
In mu-tual love our hearts u - nite.

Come to cre - ate, re - new, in - spire;
Pro - tec - tor in the midst of strife,
Teach us to speak; teach us to hear;
Your pow'r the whole cre - a - tion fills;

Come, kin-dle in our hearts your fire.
The giv - er and the Lord of life.
Yours is the tongue and yours the ear.
Con - firm our weak un - cer - tain wills.

5. From inner strife grant us release;
   Turn nations to the ways of peace.
   To fuller life your people bring
   That as one body we may sing:

6. Praise to the Father, Christ his Word,
   And to the Spirit, God the Lord;
   To whom all honor, glory be
   Both now and for eternity.

Text: *Veni, Creator Spiritus;* Attr. to Rabanus Maurus, 776-865;
   Tr. by John W. Grant, b.1919, © 1971
Tune: VENI CREATOR SPIRITUS, LM; Mode VIII; Setting by Richard J. Wojcik, b.1923
   © 1975, GIA Publications, Inc.

169

O Sons and Daughters

Al - le - lu - ia,   al - le - lu - ia,   al - le - lu - ia.

1. O   sons and daugh - ters, let   us   sing!
2. That Eas - ter morn, at   break   of   day,
3. An   an - gel clad   in   white   they see,
4. That night the a - pos - tles met   in   fear;
5. When Thom-as, first   the   ti - dings heard,

The King   of   heav'n, the glo - rious King,
The faith - ful   wom - en went   their way
Who sat,   and   spoke un - to   the three,
A - midst them came   their Lord   most dear,
How they had   seen   the ris - en Lord,

D.C.

O'er death to - day rose tri - umph-ing. Al - le - lu - ia!
To   seek the   tomb where Je - sus lay. Al - le - lu - ia!
"Your Lord has gone to   Gal - i - lee." Al - le - lu - ia!
And said, "My peace be   on   all here." Al - le - lu - ia!
He doubt - ed the   dis - ci - ples' word. Al - le - lu - ia!

6. "My wounded side, O Thomas, see;
   Behold my hands, my feet," said he,
   "Not faithless, but believing be." Alleluia!

7. No longer Thomas then denied,
   He saw the feet, the hands, the side;
   "You are my Lord and God," he cried. Alleluia!

8. How blest are they who have not seen,
   And yet whose faith has constant been,
   For they eternal life shall win. Alleluia!

9. On this most holy day of days,
   To God your hearts and voices raise,
   In laud, and jubilee and praise. Alleluia!

Text: *O filii et filiae;* Jean Tisserand, d.1494; Tr. by John M. Neale, 1818-1866, alt.
Tune: O FILII ET FILIAE, 888 with alleluias; Mode II; Acc. by Richard Proulx, b.1937
   © 1975, GIA Publications, Inc.

O Sun of Justice

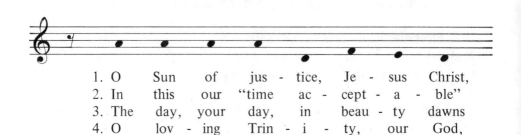

```
1. O      Sun    of    jus - tice,  Je - sus  Christ,
2. In     this   our   "time  ac - cept - a - ble"
3. The    day,   your  day,   in    beau - ty  dawns
4. O      lov - ing    Trin - i - ty,   our    God,
```

```
Dis - pel   the    dark - ness   of    our    hearts,
Touch ev - 'ry    heart  with    sor - row,   Lord,
When  in    your   light  earth   blooms a -   new;
To    you   we     bow    through end - less  days,
```

```
Till   your    blest   light   makes   night - time   flee
That, turned from sin,    re - newed  by      grace,
Led    back    a -     gain    to      life's  true    way,
And    in      your    grace   new - born      we      sing
```

```
And   brings   the    joys    your    day     im - parts.
We     may     press  on      toward  love's  re - ward.
May    we,     for - giv'n,    re -    joice   in      you.
New   hymns    of     grat - i -      tude    and     praise.
```

Text: *Jam Christe sol justitiae;* Latin, 6th C.; Tr. by Peter J. Scagnelli, b.1949, ©
Tune: JESU DULCIS MEMORIA, LM; Mode I; Acc. by Richard Proulx, b.1937
© 1975, GIA Publications, Inc.

Praise God from Whom All Blessings Flow

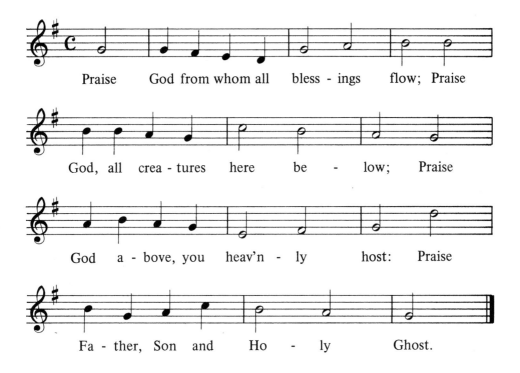

Praise God from whom all bless - ings flow; Praise
God, all crea - tures here be - low; Praise
God a - bove, you heav'n - ly host: Praise
Fa - ther, Son and Ho - ly Ghost.

Text: Doxology, adapt. by Thomas Ken, 1637-1711
Tune: OLD HUNDREDTH, LM; Louis Bourgeois, c.1510-1561

Prepare the Way of the Lord

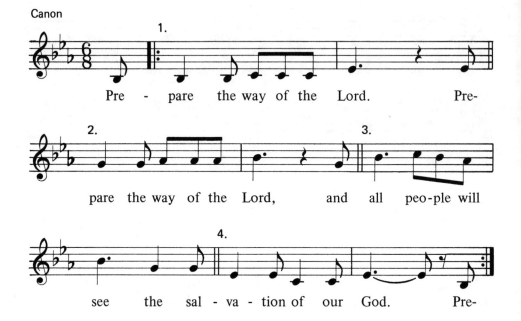

Canon

Pre - pare the way of the Lord. Pre-

pare the way of the Lord, and all peo-ple will

see the sal - va - tion of our God. Pre-

Text: Luke 3:4,6; Taizé Community, 1984
Tune: Jacques Berthier, b.1923
© 1984, Les Presses de Taizé

Seek Ye First the Kingdom of God

1. Seek ye first the king-dom of God
2. Ask, and it shall be giv-en un-to you,

and his right - eous - ness,
seek, and ye shall find,

and all these things shall be add-ed un-to you;
knock, and the door shall be o-pened un-to you;

Al - le - lu, al-le-lu - ia. Al - le-

lu - ia, al - le - lu - ia, al - le-

lu - ia, al-le - lu, al-le-lu - ia.

Text: Mt. 6:33, 7:7; St. 1, adapt. by Karen Lafferty, b.1948; St. 2, anon.
Tune: SEEK YE FIRST, Irregular; Karen Lafferty, b.1948
© 1972, Maranatha! Music

Send Us Your Spirit

Come, Lord   Je - sus,   send us your   Spir - it, re-
new   the   face   of the   earth.

Come, Lord   Je - sus,   send us your   Spir - it, re-
new   the   face   of the   earth.

Verses

1. Come   to us, Spir - it of   God,   breathe in us
2. Fill us with the fire of your love,   burn in us
3. Send   us the wings of new   birth,   fill all the

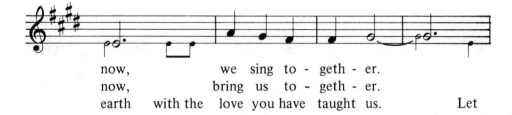

now,   we sing to - geth - er.
now,   bring us to - geth - er.
earth   with the   love you have taught us.   Let

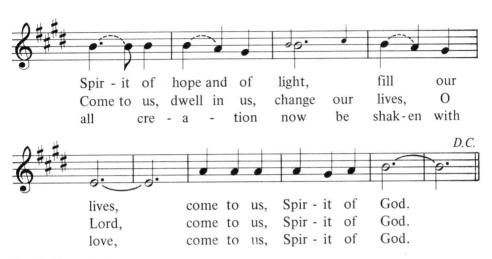

Spir - it of hope and of light, fill our
Come to us, dwell in us, change our lives, O
all cre - a - tion now be shak-en with

D.C.

lives, come to us, Spir - it of God.
Lord, come to us, Spir - it of God.
love, come to us, Spir - it of God.

Text: David Haas, b.1957
Tune: David Haas, b.1957; Acc. by Jeanne Cotter
© 1981, 1982 GIA Publications, Inc.

Shalom Chaverim

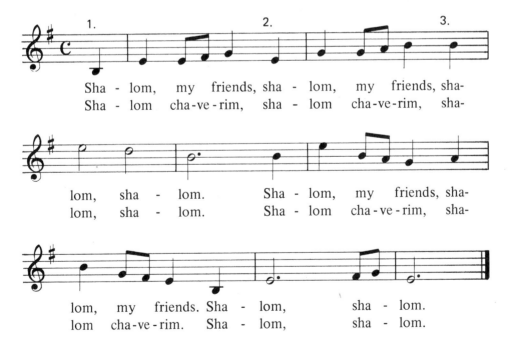

Sha - lom, my friends, sha - lom, my friends, sha-
Sha - lom cha-ve-rim, sha - lom cha-ve-rim, sha-

lom, sha - lom. Sha - lom, my friends, shalom, sha - lom. Sha - lom cha-ve-rim, sha-

lom, my friends. Sha - lom, sha - lom.
lom cha-ve-rim. Sha - lom, sha - lom.

Text: Traditional Hebrew
Tune: SHALOM CHAVERIM, Traditional Hebrew

177

Shout for Joy, Loud and Long

1. Shout for joy, loud and long, God be praised
2. By God's word all was made, Heav'n and earth,
3. Yet our pride makes us fall! So Christ came
4. Now has Christ tru - ly ris'n And his spir-

with a song! To the Lord we be - long—
light and shade, Na - ture's won - ders dis - played,
for us all— Not the right - eous to call—
it is giv'n To all those un - der heav'n

Chil - dren of our Mak - er, God the great life-
We to rule cre - a - tion From its first foun-
By his cross and pas - sion, Bring - ing us sal-
Who will walk be - side him, Though they once de-

giv - er! Shout for joy, joy, joy! Shout for joy, joy, joy!
da - tion. Shout for joy, joy, joy! Shout for joy, joy, joy!
va - tion! Shout for joy, joy, joy! Shout for joy, joy, joy!
nied him! Shout for joy, joy, joy! Shout for joy, joy, joy!

God is love, God is light, God is ev - er - last - ing!
God is love, God is light, God is ev - er - last - ing!
God is love, God is light, God is ev - er - last - ing!
God is love, God is light, God is ev - er - last - ing!

Text: David Mowbray, b.1938, © 1982, Hope Publishing Co.
Tune: PERSONET HODIE, 666 66 with refrain; *Piae Cantiones*, 1582;
Harm. by Richard Proulx, b.1937, © 1978, GIA Publications, Inc.

Sing a New Song

1. Sing a new song to the Lord,
2. Now to the ends of the earth
3. Sing a new song and re - joice,
4. Join with the hills and the sea

He to whom won - ders be - long!
See his sal - va - tion is shown;
Pub - lish his prais - es a - broad!
Thun - ders of praise to pro - long!

Re - joice in his tri - umph and
And still he re - mem- bers his
Let voic-es in cho - rus, with
In judge-ment and jus - tice he

tell of his power,
mer - cy and truth,
trum-pet and horn,
comes to the earth,

O sing to the Lord a new song!
Un - chang - ing in love to his own.
Re - sound for the joy of the Lord!
O sing to the Lord a new song!

Text: Psalm 98; Timothy Dudley-Smith, b.1926
Tune: CANTATE DOMINO, Irregular; David G. Wilson, b.1940
© 1973, Hope Publishing Co.

Sing of Mary, Pure and Lowly

1. Sing of Mar - y, pure and low - ly,
2. Sing of Je - sus, son of Mar - y,
3. Glo - ry be to God the Fa - ther;

Vir - gin - moth - er un - de - filed, Sing of God's own
In the home at Naz - a - reth. Toil and la - bor
Glo - ry be to God the Son; Glo - ry be to

Son most ho - ly, Who be - came her lit - tle child.
can - not wea - ry Love en - dur - ing un - to death.
God the Spir - it; Glo - ry to the Three in One.

Fair - est child of fair - est moth - er,
Con - stant was the love he gave her,
From the heart of bless - ed Mar - y,

God the Lord who came to earth, Word made flesh, our
Though he went forth from her side, Forth to preach, and
From all saints the song as - cends, And the church the

ver - y broth-er,   Takes our na - ture by his birth.
heal, and suf - fer,   Till on Cal - va - ry he died.
strain re - ech - oes   Un - to earth's re - mot - est ends.

Text: Roland F. Palmer, b.1891
Tune: PLEADING SAVIOR, 8 7 8 7 D; *Christian Lyre,* 1830

Sing Out, Earth and Skies

Cantor:

1. Come, O God of all the earth:
2. Come, O God of wind and flame:
3. Come, O God of flash - ing light:
4. Come, O God of snow and rain:
5. Come, O Jus - tice, Come, O Peace:

All: *Cantor:*

Come to us, O Right-eous One; Come, and bring our
Fill the earth with right-eous-ness; Teach us all to
Twin - kling star and burn - ing sun; God of day and
Show - er down up on the earth; Come, O God of
Come and shape our hearts a - new; Come and make op-

All:

love to birth: In the glo - ry of your Son.
sing your name: May our lives your love con - fess.
God of night: In your light we all are one.
joy and pain: God of sor - row, God of mirth.
pres - sion cease: Bring us all to life in you.

Sing out, earth and skies! Sing of the God who

loves you! Raise your joy - ful cries!

Dance to the life a - round you!

Text: Marty Haugen, b.1950
Tune: SING OUT, 77 77 with refrain; Marty Haugen, b.1950
© 1985, GIA Publications, Inc.

Sing with All the Saints in Glory

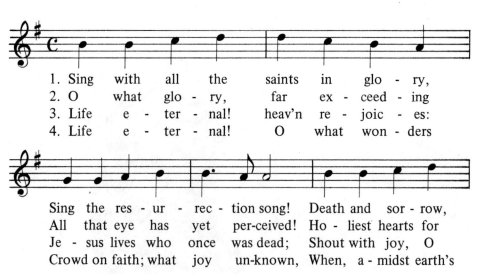

1. Sing with all the saints in glo - ry,
2. O what glo - ry, far ex - ceed - ing
3. Life e - ter - nal! heav'n re - joic - es:
4. Life e - ter - nal! O what won - ders

Sing the res - ur - rec - tion song! Death and sor - row,
All that eye has yet per-ceived! Ho - liest hearts for
Je - sus lives who once was dead; Shout with joy, O
Crowd on faith; what joy un-known, When, a - midst earth's

earth's dark sto - ry, To the for - mer
a - ges plead - ing, Nev - er that full
death - less voic - es! Child of God, lift
clos - ing thun - ders, Saints shall stand be-

days be - long. All a - round the clouds are break - ing,
joy con-ceived. God has prom-ised, Christ pre - pares it,
up your head! Pa - tri-archs from dis - tant a - ges,
fore the throne! O to en - ter that bright por - tal,

Soon the storms of time shall cease; In God's like - ness,
There on high our wel - come waits; Ev - 'ry hum - ble
Saints all long - ing for their heaven, Proph-ets, psalm-ists,
See that glow - ing fir - ma - ment, Know, with you, O

we a - wak - en, Know-ing ev - er - last - ing peace.
spir - it shares it, Christ has passed the e - ter - nal gates.
seers, and sag - es, All a - wait the glo - ry giv'n.
God im - mor - tal, "Je - sus Christ whom you have sent!"

Text: 1 Cor. 15:20; William J. Irons, 1812-1883, alt.
Tune: HYMN TO JOY, 8 7 8 7 D; Arr. from Ludwig van Beethoven, 1770-1827,
      by Edward Hodges, 1796-1867

Somebody's Knockin' at Your Door

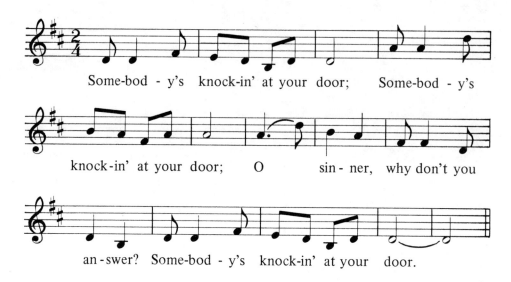

Some-bod - y's knock-in' at your door; Some-bod - y's knock-in' at your door; O sin - ner, why don't you an - swer? Some-bod - y's knock-in' at your door.

1. Knocks like Je - sus,
2. Can't you hear him? Some-bod - y's knock-in' at your
3. Je - sus calls you,
4. Can't you trust him?

Knocks like Je - sus,
door; Can't you hear him? Some-bod - y's
Je - sus calls you,
Can't you trust him?

knock-in' at your door. O sin - ner, why don't you

an - swer? Some-bod - y's knock-in' at your door.

Text: Afro-American Spiritual
Tune: SOMEBODY'S KNOCKIN', Irregular; Afro-American Spiritual;
    Harm. by Richard Proulx, b.1937, © 1986, GIA Publications, Inc.

Songs of Thankfulness and Praise

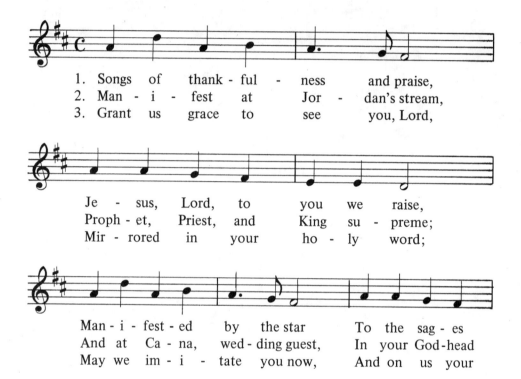

1. Songs of thank - ful - ness and praise,
2. Man - i - fest at Jor - dan's stream,
3. Grant us grace to see you, Lord,

Je - sus, Lord, to you we raise,
Proph - et, Priest, and King su - preme;
Mir - rored in your ho - ly word;

Man - i - fest - ed by the star To the sag - es
And at Ca - na, wed - ding guest, In your God - head
May we im - i - tate you now, And on us your

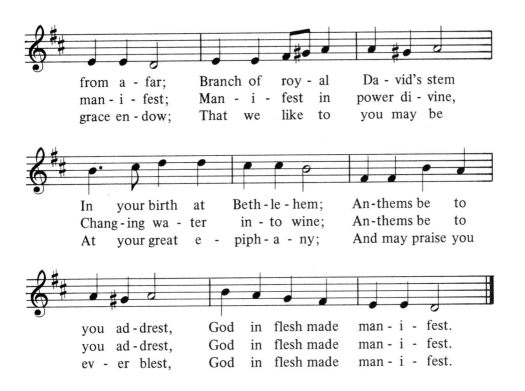

from a - far;	Branch of roy - al	Da - vid's stem	
man - i - fest;	Man - i - fest in	power di - vine,	
grace en - dow;	That we like to	you may be	

In your birth at	Beth - le - hem;	An - thems be to	
Chang - ing wa - ter	in - to wine;	An - thems be to	
At your great e -	piph - a - ny;	And may praise you	

you ad - drest,	God in flesh made	man - i - fest.	
you ad - drest,	God in flesh made	man - i - fest.	
ev - er blest,	God in flesh made	man - i - fest.	

Text: Christopher Wordsworth, 1807-1885
Tune: SALZBURG, 77 77 D; Jakob Hintze, 1622-1702, alt.; Harm. by J. S. Bach, 1685-1750

Soon and Very Soon

1. Soon and ver - y soon   we are
2. No more cry - in' there   we are
3. No more dy - in' there   we are
4. Soon and ver - y soon   we are

goin' to see the King.   Soon and ver - y soon
goin' to see the King.   No more cry - in' there
goin' to see the King.   No more dy - in' there
goin' to see the King.   Soon and ver - y soon

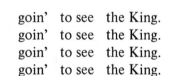

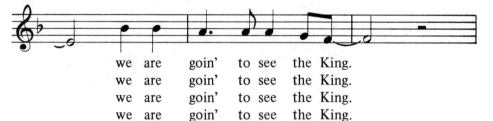

we are goin' to see the King.
we are goin' to see the King.
we are goin' to see the King.
we are goin' to see the King.

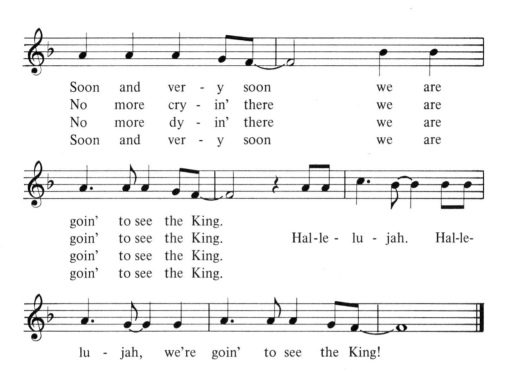

Soon and ver - y soon we are
No more cry - in' there we are
No more dy - in' there we are
Soon and ver - y soon we are

goin' to see the King.
goin' to see the King.   Hal-le - lu - jah.   Hal-le-
goin' to see the King.
goin' to see the King.

lu - jah, we're goin' to see the King!

Text: Andraé Crouch
Tune: Andraé Crouch

That Easter Day with Joy Was Bright

1. That East - er day with joy was bright,
2. His ris - en flesh with ra - diance glowed;
3. O Je - sus, King of gen - tle - ness,
4. O Lord of all, with us a - bide
5. All praise, to you, O ris - en Lord,

The sun shone out with fair - er light,
His wound - ed hands and feet he showed;
Who with your grace our hearts pos - sess
In this our joy - ful East - er - tide;
Now both by heaven and earth a - dored;

When to their long - ing eyes re - stored,
Those scars their sol - emn wit - ness gave
That we may give you all our days
From ev - 'ry weap - on death can wield
To God the Fa - ther e - qual praise,

The a - pos - tles saw their ris - en Lord.
That Christ was ris - en from the grave.
The will - ing trib - ute of our praise.
Your own re - deemed for ev - er shield.
And Spir - it blest, our songs we raise.

Text: *Claro paschali gaudio;* Latin 5th C.; Tr. by John M. Neale, 1818-1866, alt.
Tune: PUER NOBIS, LM; Adapt. by Michael Praetorius, 1571-1621

The King of Glory

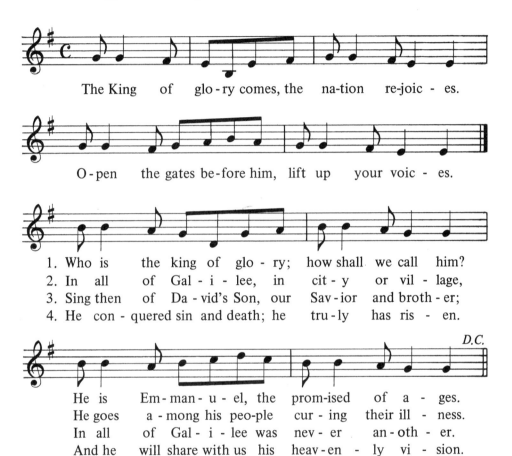

The King of glo-ry comes, the na-tion re-joic - es.

O-pen the gates be-fore him, lift up your voic - es.

1. Who is the king of glo - ry; how shall we call him?
2. In all of Gal - i - lee, in cit - y or vil - lage,
3. Sing then of Da - vid's Son, our Sav - ior and broth - er;
4. He con - quered sin and death; he tru - ly has ris - en.

D.C.

He is Em - man - u - el, the prom-ised of a - ges.
He goes a - mong his peo-ple cur - ing their ill - ness.
In all of Gal - i - lee was nev - er an - oth - er.
And he will share with us his heav - en - ly vi - sion.

Text: Willard F. Jabusch, b.1930, © 1966, 1984
Tune: KING OF GLORY, 12 12 with refrain; Israeli; Harm. by Richard Proulx, b.1937
    © 1986, GIA Publications, Inc.

The Lord, the Lord, the Lord Is My Shepherd

1. The Lord, the Lord, the Lord is my shep-herd, The
2. You bring me rest in green, green pas-tures, You
3. My fear is gone for you are with me, Your

Lord, the Lord, the Lord is my shep-herd, The
lead me to the still, still wa-ters, You
rod and staff bring com - fort sure; Your

Lord, the Lord, the Lord is my shep-herd, The
guide me a - long your own right way, The
good-ness and mer-cy shall fol - low me, The

Lord is my shep-herd and I shall not want.
Lord is my shep-herd and I shall not want.
Lord is my shep-herd and I shall not want.

Text: Afro-American Spiritual
Tune: THE LORD IS MY SHEPHERD, Irregular; Afro-American Spiritual;
    Harm. by Austin C. Lovelace, b. 1919, © 1986, GIA Publications, Inc.

This Is the Feast Day of the Lord's True Witness

1. This is the feast day of the Lord's true wit - ness, Who on this day re - ceived the glo - ry due him. Let all cre - a - tion cel - e - brate his good - ness, Cher - ish his mem - 'ry.

2. Pru - dent in judg - ment, gen - tle toward all oth - ers, O - pen, un - self - ish in the love he of - fered. All of his days the Gos - pel was his wis - dom, Christ his true teach - er.

3. Broth - er was he to all the world's for - got - ten; Lone - ly and ill, they came to him for heal - ing. God gave him pow - er, gifts for our sal - va - tion: Love, health, and par - don.

Text: *Iste confessor Domini, colentes;* Latin, 8th C.; Tr. by Peter J. Scagnelli, b.1949, ©
Tune: ISTE CONFESSOR, 11 11 11 5; Rouen Church Melody;
Harm. by Carl Schalk, b.1929, © 1969, Condordia Publishing House

This Little Light of Mine

This lit-tle light of mine, I'm gon-na let it shine, this lit-tle light of mine, I'm gon-na let it shine, this lit-tle light of mine, I'm gon-na let it shine, let it shine, let it shine, let it shine.

Text: Afro-American Spiritual
Tune: Afro-American Spiritual
    Arr. by Robert J. Batastini, b.1942, © 1988, GIA Publications, Inc.

Ubi Caritas

U - bi ca - ri - tas et a - mor,
u - bi ca - ri - tas De - us i - bi est.

Text: 1 Cor. 13:2-8, *Where charity and love are found, God is there.*
    Taizé Community, 1978
Tune: Jacques Berthier, b.1923
© 1979, Les Presses de Taizé

Veni Sancte Spiritus

Ve - ni San - cte Spi - ri - tus.

* Either octave may be sung.

Text: *Come Holy Spirit;* Verses drawn from the Pentecost Sequence;
    Taizé Community, 1978
Tune: Jacques Berthier, b.1923
© 1979, Les Presses de Taizé

Watch for Messiah

1. Light one can - dle to watch for Mes - si - ah;
2. Light two can - dles to watch for Mes - si - ah;
3. Light three can - dles to watch for Mes - si - ah;
4. Light four can - dles to watch for Mes - si - ah;

let the light ban - ish dark - ness.
let the light ban - ish dark - ness.
let the light ban - ish dark - ness.
let the light ban - ish dark - ness.

He shall bring sal - va - tion to Is-ra - el,
He shall feed his flock like a shep - herd,
Lift your heads and lift high the gate - way,
He is com - ing, tell the glad tid - ings,

God ful - fills the prom - ise.
gen - tly lead them home - ward.
for the King of Glo - ry.
let your lights be shin - ing.

Text: Wayne L. Wold
Tune: TIF IN VELDELE, 10 7 10 6; Yiddish; Arr. by Wayne L. Wold
© 1984, Fortress Press

We Are Walking in the Light

We are walk - ing in the light,

in the light, in the light, We are walk - ing

in the light, in the light of God.

Text: Traditional
Tune: James Moore, Jr., © 1987, GIA Publications, Inc.

We Remember

Refrain

We re - mem-ber how you loved us to your

death, and still we cel - e-brate, for you are with us

here; and we be - lieve that we will

see you   when you   come,   in your

glo-ry, Lord.   We re - mem - ber,   we

cel - e -brate,   we be - lieve.

Text: Marty Haugen, b.1950
Tune: Marty Haugen, b.1950
© 1980, GIA Publications, Inc.

We See the Lord

1. We see the Lord, we see the
2. We see the Lord, we see the
3. We hear the Lord, we hear the
4. We bless the Lord, we bless the

Lord, and he is high and lift - ed up, and his
Lord, and God's face shines forth as a
Lord, and God's Word is - sues forth and re-
Lord, and as in - cense goes up, so our

train fills the Tem-ple, he is high and lift - ed
light in the Tem-ple, and God's face shines
sounds through the Tem-ple, and God's Word is - sues
prayers fill the Tem-ple, and as in - cense goes

up, and his train fills the Tem-ple. The
forth as a light in the Tem-ple. The
forth and re - sounds through the Tem-ple. The
up, so our prayers fill the Tem-ple. The

an-gels cry, "Ho - ly." The an-gels cry, "Ho-ly." The
ser-aphs cry, "Worth-y." The ser-aphs cry, "Worth-y." The
el-ders cry, "A - men." The el-ders cry, "A-men." The
peo-ple cry, "Glo - ry." The peo-ple cry, "Glo-ry." The

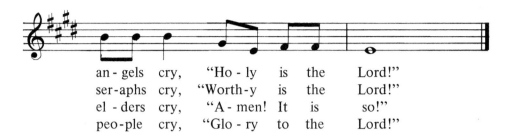

an - gels	cry,	"Ho - ly	is	the	Lord!"
ser -aphs	cry,	"Worth-y	is	the	Lord!"
el - ders	cry,	"A - men!	It	is	so!"
peo -ple	cry,	"Glo - ry	to	the	Lord!"

Text: Vs. 1, Is. 6:1-3; Vs. 2-4, James E. Byrne, © 1973
Tune: Traditional; Arr. by Charles High, © 1978, The Word of God

We Shall Overcome

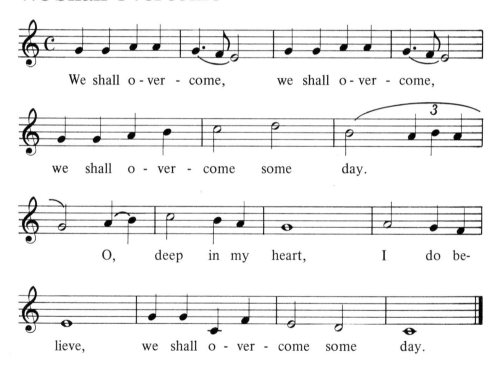

We shall o - ver - come, we shall o - ver - come,

we shall o - ver - come some day.

O, deep in my heart, I do be-

lieve, we shall o - ver - come some day.

We'll walk hand in hand . . .

We shall all have peace . . .

We are not afraid . . . today.

Text: Traditional
Tune: Traditional; Harm. by J. Jefferson Cleveland, b.1937, from *Songs of Zion*
     © 1981, by Abingdon

We Walk by Faith

1., 5. We walk by faith, and not by sight: No
2. We may not touch his hands and side, Nor
3. Help then, O Lord, our un-be-lief, And
4. That when our life of faith is done In

gra-cious words we hear Of him who spoke as
fol-low where he trod; Yet in his prom-ise
may our faith a-bound; To call on you when
realms of clear-er light We may be-hold you

none e'er spoke, But we be-lieve him near.
we re-joice, And cry "My Lord and God!"
you are near, And seek where you are found:
as you are In full and end-less sight.

Text: Henry Alford, 1810-1871, alt.
Tune: SHANTI, CM; Marty Haugen, b.1950, © 1984, GIA Publications, Inc.

Were You There

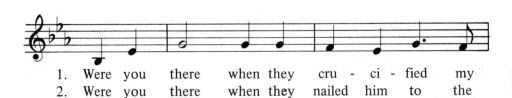

1. Were you there when they cru-ci-fied my
2. Were you there when they nailed him to the

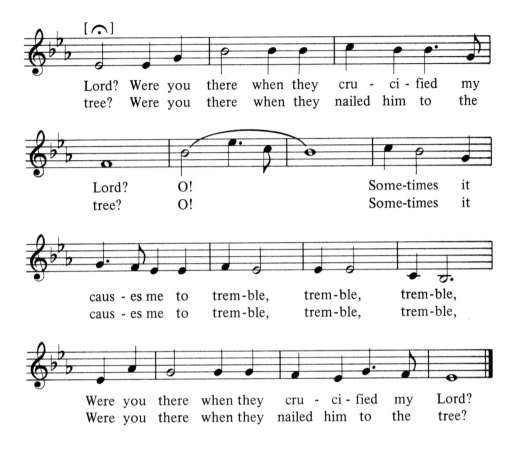

[⌢]

Lord? Were you there when they cru - ci - fied my
tree? Were you there when they nailed him to the

Lord? O! Some-times it
tree? O! Some-times it

caus - es me to trem-ble, trem-ble, trem-ble,
caus - es me to trem-ble, trem-ble, trem-ble,

Were you there when they cru - ci - fied my Lord?
Were you there when they nailed him to the tree?

3. Were you there when they laid him in the tomb?
Were you there when they laid him in the tomb?
O! Sometimes it causes me to tremble, tremble, tremble,
Were you there when they laid him in the tomb?

4. Were you there when they rolled the stone away?
Were you there when they rolled the stone away?
O! Sometimes it causes me to tremble, tremble, tremble,
Were you there when they rolled the stone away?

Text: Afro-American Spiritual
Tune: WERE YOU THERE, 10 10 with refrain; Afro-American Spiritual;
    Harm. by C. Winfred Douglas, 1867-1944
    © 1940, 1943, 1961, Church Pension Fund

What Child Is This

1. What child is this, who, laid to rest, On
2. Why lies he in such mean es - tate Where
3. So bring him in - cense, gold, and myrrh, Come,

Mar - y's lap is sleep - ing? Whom
ox and ass are feed - ing? Good
peas - ant, king to own him; The

an - gels greet with an - thems sweet, While
Chris - tian, fear; for sin - ners here The
King of kings sal - va - tion brings, Let

shep - herds watch are keep - ing?
si - lent Word is plead - ing.
lov - ing hearts en - throne him.

This, this is Christ the King, Whom

shep - herds guard and an - gels sing; Haste, haste to

bring him laud, The babe, the Son of Mar - y.

Text: William C. Dix, 1827-1898
Tune: GREENSLEEVES, 8 7 8 7 with refrain; English Melody, 16th C.;
     Harm. by John Stainer, 1840-1901

What Wondrous Love Is This

1. What won-drous love is this, O my soul, O my
2. To God and to the Lamb I will sing, I will
3. And when from death I'm free, I'll sing on, I'll sing

soul? What won - drous love is this, O my
sing; To God and to the Lamb, I will
on; And when from death I'm free, I'll sing

soul? What won-drous love is this that
sing; To God and to the Lamb who
on; And when from death I'm free, I'll

caused the Lord of bliss To bear the dread - ful
is the great I Am, While mil - lions join the
sing and joy - ful be, And through e - ter - ni-

curse for my soul, for my soul; To
theme, I will sing, I will sing; While
ty I'll sing on, I'll sing on! And

bear   the   dread - ful   curse   for   my   soul?
mil - lions join   the   theme,   I   will   sing.
through e - ter - ni - ty,   I'll   sing   on.

Text: Alexander Means, 1801-1853
Tune: WONDROUS LOVE, 12 9 12 12 9; *Southern Harmony,* 1835;
    Harm. from *Cantate Domino, 1980,* © 1980, World Council of Churches

Ye Watchers and Ye Holy Ones

1. Ye watch - ers and ye ho - ly ones,
2. O high - er than the cher - u - bim,
3. Re - spond, ye souls in end - less rest,
4. O friends, in glad - ness let us sing,

Bright ser - aphs, cher - u - bim, and thrones,
More glo - rious than the ser - a - phim,
Ye pa - tri - archs and proph-ets blest,
Su - per - nal an - thems ech - o - ing,

Raise the glad strain, Al - le - lu - ia!
Lead their prais - es, Al - le - lu - ia!
Al - le - lu - ia, Al - le - lu - ia!
Al - le - lu - ia, Al - le - lu - ia!

Cry out, do - min - ions, prince-doms, powers,
O bear - er of the e - ter - nal Word,
Ye ho - ly Twelve, ye mar - tyrs strong,
To God the Fa - ther, God the Son,

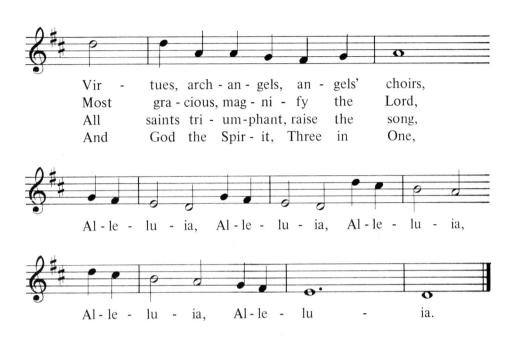

Vir - tues, arch - an - gels, an - gels' choirs,
Most gra - cious, mag - ni - fy the Lord,
All saints tri - um - phant, raise the song,
And God the Spir - it, Three in One,

Al - le - lu - ia, Al - le - lu - ia, Al - le - lu - ia,

Al - le - lu - ia, Al - le - lu - ia.

Text: John A. Riley, 1858-1945; © Oxford University Press
Tune: LASST UNS ERFREUEN, LM with alleluias; *Geistliche Kirchengesänge*, Cologne,
   1623; Harm. by Ralph Vaughan Williams, 1872-1958, © Oxford University Press

You Have Put on Christ

Cantor, then All:

You have put on Christ, in him you have been bap-

tized. Al - le - lu - ia, al - le - lu - ia.

Text: From the *Rite of Baptism for Children*
   © 1969, International Committee on English in the Liturgy, Inc. (ICEL)
Tune: Howard Hughes, S.M., from *Music for Rite of Funerals and*
   Rite of Baptism for Children, © 1977, ICEL, Inc.

...

Prayers

The Lord's Prayer

Jesus' friends once asked him to teach them to pray. He taught them the prayer that begins "Our Father." This prayer belongs to every Christian. We pray it every day and especially on Sunday. The words are found on page 10.

Doxology

Glory to the Father, and to the Son, and to the Holy Spirit: as it was in the beginning, is now, and will be for ever. Amen.

Prayers to Mary

A ▪ Hail Mary, full of grace,
the Lord is with you!
Blessed are you among women,
and blessed is the fruit of your womb, Jesus.
Holy Mary, mother of God,
pray for us sinners,
now and at the hour of our death. Amen.

The "Angelus" is prayed at noon and at six in the evening every day:

B ▪ The angel spoke God's message to Mary,
and she conceived of the Holy Spirit.
Hail Mary. . .

"I am the lowly servant of the Lord:
let it be done to me according to your word."
Hail Mary. . .

And the Word became flesh
and lived among us.
Hail Mary. . .

Pray for us, holy Mother of God,
that we may become worthy of the promises of Christ.

Let us pray.

Lord,
fill our hearts with your grace:
once, through the message of an angel
you revealed to us the incarnation of your Son;
now, through his suffering and death
lead us to the glory of his resurrection.
We ask this through Christ our Lord. Amen.

C ▪ Mary, mother whom we bless,
full of grace and tenderness,
defend me from the devil's power
and greet me in my dying hour.

D ▪ We turn to you for protection,
holy Mother of God.
Listen to our prayers
and help us in our needs.
Save us from every danger,
glorious and blessed virgin.

Meal Prayers

A ▪ Bless us, O Lord, and these your gifts
which we are about to receive from your goodness.
Through Christ our Lord. Amen.

Another way of praying this blessing:

Bless us, O Lord, and these thy gifts
which we are about to receive from thy bounty.
Through Christ our Lord. Amen.

B ▪ Lord, the lover of life,
  you feed the birds of the skies
  and array the lilies of the field.
  We bless you for all your creatures
  and for the food we are about to receive.
  We humbly pray that in your goodness
  you will provide for our brothers and sisters
  who are suffering hunger.
  We ask this through Christ our Lord. Amen.

This blessing may be sung:

C ▪ Be present at our table, Lord.
  Be here and everywhere adored.
  Thy creatures bless and grant that we
  May feast in Paradise with thee.

D ▪ We give you thanks for all your gifts, almighty God,
  living and reigning now and for ever. Amen.

E ▪ The eyes of all creatures look to you
  to give them food in due time.
  You give it to them, they gather it up;
  you open your hand, they have their fill.
  FROM PSALM 104

F ▪ May your gifts refresh us, O Lord,
  and your grace give us strength. Amen.

Night Prayers

A ▪ May the all-powerful Lord grant us a restful night
  and a peaceful death.

B ▪ Keep us, Lord, as the apple of your eye
  and shelter us in the shadow of your wing.

C ▪ Angel sent by God to guide me,
    be my light and walk beside me;
    be my guardian and protect me;
    on the paths of life direct me.

D ▪ Protect us, Lord, as we stay awake;
    watch over us as we sleep,
    that awake, we may keep watch with Christ,
    and asleep, rest in his peace. Amen.

Prayer of Contrition

▪ My God,
    I am sorry for my sins with all my heart.
    In choosing to do wrong
    and failing to do good,
    I have sinned against you
    whom I should love above all things.
    I firmly intend, with your help,
    to do penance,
    to sin no more,
    and to avoid whatever leads me to sin.

Our Savior Jesus Christ
suffered and died for us.
In his name, my God, have mercy.

▪ Lord Jesus, Son of God,
    have mercy on me, a sinner.

Short Prayers

A ▪ Come, Lord Jesus!

B ▪ We adore you, O Christ, and we bless you:
   because by your holy cross you have redeemed
      the world.

C ▪ Come, Holy Spirit, fill the hearts of your faithful.
   And kindle in them the fire of your love.

D ▪ Hear us, Lord,
   and send your angel from heaven
   to visit and protect,
   to comfort and defend
   all who live in this house. Amen.

For those who have died:

E ▪ Eternal rest grant unto them, O Lord.
   And let perpetual light shine upon them.
   May they rest in peace. Amen.

Scripture Readings for Daily Prayer

To Begin the Day

A ▪ Listen to the words of the book of Genesis.
   God said, "Let there be lights in the dome of the sky,
   to separate day from night." And so it happened: God
   made the two great lights, the greater one to govern
   the day, and the lesser one to govern the night; and
   God made the stars. God set them in the dome of the
   sky, to shed light upon the earth.
   GENESIS 1:14, 15–16

B ▪ Listen to the words of the book of Genesis.
God said, "Let the earth bring forth all kinds of living creatures: cattle, creeping things, and wild animals of all kinds." And so it happened: God made all kinds of wild animals, all kinds of cattle, and all kinds of creeping things of the earth. God saw how good it was.
GENESIS 1:24–25

C ▪ Listen to the words of Paul.
Rejoice with those who rejoice, weep with those who weep. Do not repay anyone evil for evil; be concerned for what is noble in the sight of all. If possible, on your part, live at peace with all. Do not be conquered by evil but conquer evil with good.
ROMANS 12:15, 17, 18, 21

D ▪ Listen to the words of the book of Tobit.
Do to no one what you yourself dislike. Give to the hungry some of your bread, and to the naked some of your clothing. At all times bless the Lord God, and ask him to make all your paths straight and to grant success to all your endeavors and plans.
TOBIT 4:15, 16, 19

E ▪ Listen to the words of the gospel of Luke.
There was a scholar of the law who stood up to test Jesus and said, "Teacher, what must I do to inherit eternal life?" Jesus said to him, "What is written in the law? How do you read it?" He said in reply, "You shall love the Lord, your God, with all your heart, with all your being, with all your strength, and with all your mind, and your neighbor as yourself." He replied to him, "You have answered correctly; do this and you will live."
LUKE 10:25–28

F ▪ Listen to the words of the book of Judith.
O God, your strength is not in numbers. You are the God of the lowly, the helper of the oppressed, the supporter of the weak, the protector of the forsaken, the savior of those without hope. Please, please, Lord of heaven and earth, Creator of the waters, hear my prayer!
JUDITH 9:5, 11–12

G ▪ Listen to the words of the book of Job.
Then the Lord addressed Job out of the storm:
Have you ever in your lifetime commanded the
    morning
    and shown the dawn its place?
Have you entered the storehouse of the snow,
    and seen the treasury of the hail?
Can you send forth the lightnings on their way,
    or will they say to you, 'Here we are'?
JOB 38:1, 12, 22, 35

H ▪ Listen to the words of the gospel of Matthew.
Children were brought to Jesus that he might lay his hands on them and pray. The disciples rebuked them, but Jesus said, "Let the children come to me, and do not prevent them; for the kingdom of heaven belongs to such as these." After he placed his hands on them, he went away.
MATTHEW 19:13–15

To End the Day

A ▪ Listen to the words of Paul.
This is my prayer: that your love may increase ever more and more in knowledge and every kind of perception, to discern what is of value, so that you may be pure and blameless for the day of Christ, filled with the fruit of righteousness that comes through Jesus Christ for the glory and praise of God.
PHILIPPIANS 1:9–11

B ▪ Listen to the words of Paul.
May the Lord make you increase and abound in love for one another and for all, just as we have for you, so as to strengthen your hearts, to be blameless in holiness before our God and Father at the coming of our Lord Jesus with all his holy ones.
1 THESSALONIANS 3:12–13

C ▪ Listen to the words of Paul.
If I have all faith so as to move mountains but do not have love, I am nothing. If I give away everything I own, and if I hand my body over so that I may boast but do not have love, I gain nothing. Love is patient, love is kind. It does not rejoice over wrongdoing but rejoices with the truth. It bears all things, believes all things, hopes all things, endures all things.
1 CORINTHIANS 13:2–4, 6–7

D ▪ Listen to the words of the Acts of the Apostles.
Now Peter and John were going up to the temple area for the three o'clock hour of prayer. And a man crippled from birth was carried and placed at the gate of the temple called "the Beautiful Gate" every day to beg for alms from the people who entered the temple. When he saw Peter and John about to go into the temple, he asked for alms. But Peter looked intently at him, as did John, and said, "Look at us." He paid

attention to them, expecting to receive something
from them. Peter said, "I have neither silver nor gold,
but what I do have I give you: in the name of Jesus
Christ the Nazorean, rise and walk." Then Peter took
him by the right hand and raised him up, and
immediately his feet and ankles grew strong. He
leaped up, stood, and walked around, and went into
the temple with them, walking and jumping and
praising God.
ACTS 3:1–8

E ▪ Listen to the words of the gospel of Matthew.
Jesus said, "Love your enemies, and pray for those
who persecute you, that you may be children of your
heavenly Father, for he makes his sun rise on the bad
and the good, and causes rain to fall on the just and
the unjust."
MATTHEW 5:44–45

F ▪ Listen to the words of the prophet Isaiah.
The wolf shall be a guest of the lamb,
  and the leopard shall lie down with the kid;
The calf and the young lion shall browse together,
  with a little child to guide them.
The cow and the bear shall be neighbors,
  together their young shall rest;
  the lion shall eat hay like the ox.
There shall be no harm or ruin on all my holy
    mountain;
  for the earth shall be filled with knowledge of the LORD,
  as water covers the sea.
ISAIAH 11:6–7, 9

G ▪ Listen to the words of the prophet Micah.
You have been told what is good,
  and what the LORD requires of you:
Only to do the right and to love goodness,
  and to walk humbly with your God.
MICAH 6:8

H ■ Listen to the words of the book of Genesis.
God said: "See, I give you every seed-bearing plant all over the earth and every tree that has seed-bearing fruit on it to be your food; and to all the animals of the land, all the birds of the air, and all the living creatures that crawl on the ground, I give all the green plants for food." And so it happened. God looked at everything he had made, and he found it very good. Evening came, and morning followed — the sixth day.
GENESIS 1:29–312

Acknowledgments

The publisher gratefully acknowledges the following holders of copyright whose permission has been granted for the inclusion of material in this book. Every effort has been made to determine the ownership of all tunes, texts and harmonizations used in the edition and to make proper arrangements for their use. The publisher regrets any error or oversight which may have occurred and will readily make proper acknowledgment in future editions if such omission is made known. Acknowledgments are stated in accordance with the requirements of the individual copyright holder.

All service music and texts found from pages 3 through 95 is copyright by GIA Publications, Inc., with the exception of those texts specified on the reverse of the title page, and other items specified below. The hymn copyrights – beginning with page 99 – are specified below.

References are to page number. Where more than one title is on a page, each is noted by its composer.

4 Text: © 1969, James Quinn, SJ. By permission of Geoffrey Chapman, a division of Cassell Ltd. Harm: © A. Gregory Murray, OSB
8 Text: © 1969, James Quinn, SJ. By permission of Geoffrey Chapman, a division of Cassell Ltd.
13 Trans: © William G. Storey. Acc: © 1975, GIA Publication, Inc.
57 Gelineau: © 1963, The Grail, GIA Publications, Inc., agent
58 Murray: © 1963, The Grail, GIA Publications, Inc., agent
61 Murray: © 1963, The Grail, GIA Publications, Inc., agent
61 Gelineau: © 1963, The Grail, GIA Publications, Inc., agent
62 Howell: © 1963, The Grail, GIA Publications, Inc., agent
65 Murray: © 1963, The Grail, GIA Publications, Inc., agent
74 Taizé: Music: © 1984, Les Presses de Taizé, GIA Publications, Inc., agent
75 O'Carroll/Walker: Music: © 1985, Fintan O'Carroll and Christopher Walker. Published in England by St. Thomas More Centre, London. Published and distributed in North America by OCP Publications, Portland, OR 97213.
75 Taizé: Music: © 1980, Les Presses de Taizé, GIA Publications, Inc., agent
76 Music: © 1970, World Library Publications, Inc.
77 Music: © 1970, J. S. Paluch Company, Inc.
99 Trans: © Peter J. Scagnelli
100 Harm: © Oxford University Press
102 Harm: © 1975, GIA Publications, Inc.

108 Harm: © 1982, Hope Publishing Co., Carol Stream, IL 60188
112 Text and Music: © 1985, GIA Publications, Inc.
114 Text and Music: © 1986, GIA Publications, Inc.
118 Text and Music: © 1968, Augsburg Publishing House
120 Taizé: Text and Music: © 1984, Les Presses de Taizé, GIA Publications, Inc., agent
122 Text and Music: © 1984, Utryck, used by permission of Walton Music Corporation
124 Text and Music: © 1982, GIA Publications, Inc.
126 Text and Music: © 1977, Archdiocese of Philadelphia
128 Taizé: Text and Music: © 1979, Les Presses de Taizé, GIA Publications, Inc., agent
128 Afro-American Spiritual: Text: By permission of Mrs. John W. Work III. Music: © Walton Music Corp.
130 Text: © 1967, Hope Publishing Co. Music: © 1969, *Contemporary Worship I: Hymns*, used by permission of Augsburg Publishing House
134 Text and Music: © 1970, GIA Publications, Inc.
136 Harm: © 1986, GIA Publications, Inc.
138 Text and Music: © 1970, 1975, Celebration, Maranatha! Music, agent
140 Text: © 1971, Faber Music Ltd., London. Reprinted from *New Catholic Hymnal* by permission of the publishers.
141 Text: © American Tract Society, Garland, Texas

142 Text and Music: © 1986, Les Presses de Taizé, GIA Publications, Inc., agent

143 Text and Tune: © 1969, and Arr: © 1982 Hope Publishing Co., Carol Stream, IL 60188

145 Text and Music: © 1981, Les Presses de Taizé, GIA Publications, Inc., agent

147 Text and Music: © 1979, Les Presses de Taizé, GIA Publications, Inc., agent

150 Text: © 1939, E. C. Schirmer Music Co., Harm: The Royal School of Church Music

151 Harm: © 1986, GIA Publications, Inc.

152 Text and Music: © 1982, GIA Publications, Inc.

153 The text "Let us with joy our voices raise" has been reprinted with permission of the copyright owner, F.E.L. Publications, Ltd., 3342 S. Sandhill Rd., Suite 9-444, Las Vegas, NV 89121, Phone: (702) 737-0142. Further reproduction (even words only or one time usage) is not permitted without F.E.L.'s written permission.

154 Text and Music: © Hymns Ancient and Modern, Ltd.

155 Text: from *Enlarged Songs of Praise,* © Oxford University Press. Harm: © 1985, Hope Publishing Co., Carol Stream, IL 60188

156 Rowthorn: Text: © 1978, Hope Publishing Co., Carol Stream, IL 60188

158 Text and Music: © 1979, Les Presses de Taizé, GIA Publications, Inc., agent

160 Text and Music: © 1983, GIA Publications, Inc.

162 Harm: © A. Gregory Murray, OSB, Downside Abbey, Stratton on the Fosse, Bath, Somerset, BA3 4RH England

166 Acc: © 1975, GIA Publications, Inc.

169 Text: © 1971, John Webster Grant. Harm: © 1975, GIA Publications, Inc.

170 Acc: © 1975, GIA Publications, Inc.

172 Trans: © Peter J. Scagnelli. Acc: © 1975, GIA Publications, Inc.

174 Text and Music: © 1984, Les Presses de Taizé, GIA Publications, Inc., agent

175 Text and Music: © 1972, Maranatha! Music

176 Text and Music: © 1981, 1982, GIA Publications, Inc.

178 Text: © 1982, Hope Publishing Co., Carol Stream, IL 60188. Harm: © 1978, GIA Publications, Inc.

179 Text and Music: © 1973, Hope Publishing Co., Carol Stream, IL 60188

182 Text and Music: © 1985, GIA Publications, Inc.

186 Harm: © 1986, GIA Publications, Inc.

190 Text and Music: © 1976, Lexicon Music Inc./Crouch Music

193 Text: © 1966, 1984, Willard F. Jabusch. Harm: © 1986, GIA Publications, Inc.

194 Harm: © 1986, GIA Publications, Inc.

195 Trans: © Peter J. Scagnelli. Harm: © 1969, Concordia Publishing House

196 Arr: © 1988, GIA Publications, Inc.

197 Text and Music: © 1979, Les Presses de Taizé, GIA Publications, Inc., agent

198 Text and Harm: © 1984, Fortress Press

199 Music: © 1987, GIA Publications, Inc.

200 Text and Music: © 1980, GIA Publications, Inc.

202 Text: St. 2-4 © 1973, James E. Byrne. Arr: © 1978, The Word of God. Acc: © 1989, GIA Publications, Inc.

203 Harm: from *Songs of Zion*, © 1981, Abingdon Press

204 Haugen: Music: © 1984, GIA Publications, Inc.

204 Afro-American Spiritual: Harm: from *The Hymnal*, © 1940, 1943, 1961, Church Pension Fund

208 Harm: from *Cantate Domino, 1980,* © 1980, World Council of Churches

210 Text and Harm: from the *English Hymnal*, © Oxford University Press

211 Text: © 1969, and Music: © 1977, International Committee on English in the Liturgy, Inc.

Index of First Lines and Common Titles